# GRADUATING
*with*
# 1ST CLASS HONOURS

# GRADUATING
*with*
# 1ST CLASS HONOURS

DEREK PELL, B.ENG (HONS)

© 2010 Derek Pell

First edition published by Cambridge Academic, The Studio, High Green, Gt. Shelford, Cambridge CB2 5EG.

The rights of Derek Pell to be identified as the author of this work have been asserted by him in accordance with the Copyright, Designs and Patents Act 1988.

All rights reserved. No part of this publication may be reproduced, stored in a retrieval system, or transmitted in any form or by any means, electronic, mechanical, photocopying, recording, or otherwise without prior permission of
Cambridge Academic at:
The Studio, High Green, Gt. Shelford, Cambridge. CB2 5EG

ISBN 1-903-499-5-
978-1-903499-5-

The contents of this publication are provided in good faith and neither The Author nor The Publisher can be held responsible for any errors or omissions contained herein. Any person relying upon the information must independently satisfy himself or herself as to the safety or any other implications of acting upon such information and no liability shall be accepted either by The Author or The Publisher in the event of reliance upon such information nor for any damage or injury arising from any interpretation of its contents. This publication may not be used in any process of risk assessment.

Printed and bound in the United Kingdom by
4edge Ltd, 7a Eldon Way Industrial Estate, Hockley, Essex, SS5 4AD.

# Contents

Tables..................................................................................................i
Figures................................................................................................ii
Disclaimer.........................................................................................iii
About the Author..............................................................................iv
Tutor comments ................................................................................v

1. **Introduction**..............................................................................1
   1.1 Subject scope.......................................................................2
   1.2 Ongoing services.................................................................2
   1.3 How to use this publication.................................................3

2. **Mindset for First Class Honours**............................................5
   2.1 Enough semantics, let's be specific....................................6
       2.1.1 Employment................................................................6
       2.1.2 Treat your course seriously, it's an opportunity.........7
       2.1.3 Don't focus on how big your workload is...................8
       2.1.4 Building confidence....................................................9
       2.1.5 Collaboration............................................................10
       2.1.6 Maintain a good relationship with your lecturers....10
       2.1.7 Motivation.................................................................11
       2.1.8 Sickness or other unavoidable interruptions...........12
   2.2 Getting the balance right..................................................12

3. **Strategy for First Class Honours**.........................................15
   3.1 Treat each assessment in your workload with equal importance..........................................................................15
       3.1.1 The exception to the rule.........................................18
   3.2 Work hard: work smart......................................................19
   3.3 Multitask............................................................................22
   3.4 Thinking outside the box..................................................23
   3.5 When is an item finished?................................................25

4. **Coursework**..............................................................................27
   4.1 Backing up and saving work regularly..............................27
   4.2 How to present your coursework......................................27
       4.2.1 General Coursework assessment tips.....................29
       4.2.2 Making the most of feedback..................................31

- 4.2.3 Setting up font styles..................................................31
- 4.2.4 Essay Writing..........................................................40
  - 4.2.4.1 Research...........................................................40
  - 4.2.4.2 Structure...........................................................40
  - 4.2.4.3 Body.................................................................41
  - 4.2.4.4 Analysis............................................................42
  - 4.2.4.5 Don't digress....................................................42
  - 4.2.4.6 Style as well as substance................................42
  - 4.2.4.7 Can I write from my own perspective?.........43
- 4.2.5 Assignments...........................................................43
- 4.2.6 Preparing presentations (AKA Viva).......................50
  - 4.2.6.1 How to plan an Interim Presentation...........50
  - 4.2.6.2 How to plan a Final Presentation................52
  - 4.2.6.3 Producing and memorising verbal content..53
- 4.2.7 Exams.....................................................................54
- 4.2.8 Group Project (second year)..................................58
  - 4.2.8.1 Overview..........................................................58
  - 4.2.8.2 Assessment 1: Interim Group Presentation.65
  - 4.2.8.3 Assessment 2: Group Project Report..........67
  - 4.2.8.4 Assessment 3: Final Group Project Presentation..................................................75
  - 4.2.8.5 Accompanying files for group project...........79
- 4.2.9 Major Project (third year).......................................80
  - 4.2.9.1 Overview..........................................................80
  - 4.2.9.2 Major Project Handbook...............................81
  - 4.2.9.3 Project Proposal............................................97
  - 4.2.9.4 Assessment 1: Project Feasibility Study Report..............................................................97
  - 4.2.9.5 Assessment 2: Interim Viva Voce................98
  - 4.2.9.6 Assessment 3: Final Viva Voce..................102
  - 4.2.9.7 Assessment 4: Major Project Report.........105
    - 4.2.9.7.1 Front cover page................106
    - 4.2.9.7.2 Abstract...............................107
    - 4.2.9.7.3 Notations.............................107
    - 4.2.9.7.4 Future Work.......................107
    - 4.2.9.7.5 Referencing........................108
    - 4.2.9.7.6 Appendices........................109
    - 4.2.9.7.7 My tips for a good report.....110

        4.2.9.8 Assessment 5:Exhibition............................114

5. **Conclusion**..................................................................................**115**

6. **Notes**...........................................................................................**117**

7. **Bibliography**...............................................................................**119**

# Tables

Table 1. Why all assessments should be treated with equal importance part 1.................................................................................................16

Table 2. Why all assessments should be treated with equal importance part 2.................................................................................................18

Table 3. Settings for Heading 2..........................................................36

Table 4. Settings for Heading 3..........................................................37

Table 5. Settings for Heading 4 and 5................................................38

Table 6. Settings for Caption + Centered styles.................................39

Table 7. Areas of assessment, number of assessment vehicles and project description........................................................................................60

Table 8. Additional double sided information sheet handed out with the project brief......................................................................................61

Table 9. Accompanying files for group project...................................79

Table 10. Front page of Major Project Handbook..............................81

Table 11. Page 2 of Major Project Handbook....................................82

Table 12. Page 3 of Major Project Handbook....................................83

Table 13. Page 4 of Major Project Handbook....................................84

Table 14. Page 5 of Major Project Handbook....................................85

Table 15. Page 6 of Major Project Handbook....................................86

Table 16. Page 7 of Major Project Handbook....................................87

Table 17. Page 8 of Major Project Handbook....................................88

Table 18. Page 9 of Major Project Handbook....................................89

Table 19. Page 10 of Major Project Handbook..................................90

Table 20. Page 11 of Major Project Handbook..................................91

Table 21. Page 12 of Major Project Handbook..................................92

Table 22. Page 13 of Major Project Handbook..................................93

Table 23. Page 14 of Major Project Handbook..................................94

Table 24. Page 15 of Major Project Handbook............................................95
Table 25. Page 16 of Major Project Handbook............................................96
Table 26. Page 17 of Major Project Handbook............................................97
Table 27. Example of notations for abbreviations......................................107
Table 28. Section of a Reference page from Major Project Report...........109

# Figures

Figure 1. How your style menu will look with a new document...................31
Figure 2. How your style menu should look for assessments....................32
Figure 3. The font window showing the settings for heading 1..................32
Figure 4. The paragraph window showing the setup for heading 1............33
Figure 5. The Tabs window showing the settings for Heading 1.................34
Figure 6. The Bulleted setting for Heading 1...............................................34
Figure 7. The Numbered setting for Heading 1...........................................35
Figure 8. The Outline Numbered setting for Heading 1...............................35

# Disclaimer

The material published in 'Graduating with First Class Honours' is intended for educational and informational purposes, with the aim of being beneficial in achieving First or grade 'A' in undergraduate degrees in the UK, USA and Canada. Students following this publication are not guaranteed to achieve First Class Honours or grade 'A'. Final graduate grades are directly proportional to the depth and quality of the coursework submitted and exams completed, and hence are beyond the control of this publication and the author.

1stAcademy and the author shall have neither liability nor responsibility to any student with respect to graduating with less than First Class Honours or grade 'A' in the USA and Canada, or not graduating a degree course. Furthermore, 1stAcademy and the author shall have neither liability nor responsibility to any person or entity with respect to any loss, damage or injury, caused or alleged to be caused directly or indirectly by the information contained within this publication (this includes all accompanying files). All material included with this publication and on the associated website is protected by copyright.

# About the author

Derek Pell became interested in publishing his own work after completing his degree in June 2006 and co-publishing a paper with Dr Ian Wells of Swansea Metropolitan University based on the findings of his third year degree project.

This had been further encouraged by an early success years before, when he developed and sold his own software named ElectroCAD and later ProCAD; CAD systems programmed for the then popular Commodore Amiga. This software was sold to students and hobbyists throughout the UK and Europe.

Before graduating as a mature student with First Class Honours Derek worked in a range of industries, from software, electronics, digital TV, avionics and spacecraft communications in a combination of permanent and contract roles. His last position before beginning his degree in Computer Systems and Electronics was at EADS Astrium, the European spacecraft specialists at their site in Portsmouth, Hampshire, in which he worked on the SkyNet5 project for the MOD. At this time he was qualified to UK HNC level and had been awarded the GUY CUP in 1992 by William Lloyd, of The Isle of Wight College, for outstanding achievements in Microprocessor Interfacing.

After graduating Derek was employed by Delphi Diesel Systems Ltd (Kent) as a systems engineer and latter Radiodetection Ltd as a design engineer working with the Bristol based cable detector team prior to becoming a published author.

## Other publications

Derek Pell is also author of Bodyspy, a body language training manual presented with over 170 illustrations, and designed to gain a greater understanding of human interaction, including thought and attitude. Bodyspy also imparts how body language can be used to give the reader an edge in face-to-face negotiating such as sales, interviewing and social activities.

Bodyspy articles can currently be viewed online at:
http://www.articlesbase.com/find-articles.php?q=derek+pell

The Bodyspy Training Manual is available from:
www.bodyspyteachings.com.

# Tutor comments

### Robin Holland: Assistant Dean of Faculty

I was Assistant Dean of Faculty and I lectured to Derek Pell in microprocessor and microcontroller subjects when he completed his B.Eng with first class honours. Derek was an outstanding student. He demonstrated flair and he maintained a remarkably high level of consistency of performance in all aspects of his studies. His time management, work planning and contributions to team work were exemplary. I thoroughly recommend his guide to attaining best results in an undergraduate course. The advice he offers is astute and detailed. He has covered a wealth of study and performance techniques and has presented his ideas and advice in a thoroughly readable and interesting manner.

### Dr Ian Wells: Head of the School of Applied Computing

Derek Pell began studying at Swansea Institute in September 2004 and graduated with first class honours in B.Eng Computer Systems and Electronics in August 2006. Derek was a pupil in two subjects I tutored (including the Major Project unit) and achieved outstanding marks in both. As Head of the School of Applied Computing I verified many of Derek's assessments during the marking process and found them to be of a high standard; grades over 70% were commonplace. Throughout the duration of the course I found Derek had a methodical and consistent approach to managing his studies. He was a well organised student who took an active role in class and always met deadlines.

The author wishes to thank Chris Nightingale, Dr Ian Wells and Robin Holland for their support with the "Graduating with First Class Honours" project.

In addition thanks is given to the lecturers of Swansea Metropolitan University and the University itself for making it possible to produce this book by providing an outstanding tuition and learning experience.

# 1. Introduction

When I began my degree in 2004 I had no idea of the workload ahead. I thought I had an idea of what to expect regarding the frequency and standard of work, but with hindsight my reckoning was in error. From the beginning I wanted a First and was determined to give it my best shot. I was fairly confident, having achieved HNC level in Electrical and Electronic Engineering with a number of distinctions and merits, and I had also worked as an engineer for many years. Indeed, there was every reason to be confident, but I had underestimated the volume of assessments a full time students receives and the level of workmanship expected to gain either a lower or upper second, let alone a First.

The volume and frequency of work and the quality required are the biggest obstacles you need to overcome to gain a First. These obstacles are accountable for the majority of good students who graduate with a 2:1 or lower. The complexity of the tasks asked of students is another. For example, in my second year in Object Orientated Programming, we were asked to solve a network routing problem in the subject's only assignment. This is one of the hardest academic problems I'd ever encountered and by the time the hand-in date came over half the class had dropped out. To be fair, many never treated the course seriously and failed to attend a number of lectures. They were always going to drop out; it was just a question of when. Thus, if you want a First, you are going to need to work hard, work smart and be prepared to solve some difficult academic problems. Luckily you have some help; and believe me, management of these obstacles is tantamount to gaining a First.

If asked: "What are the main factors to achieving a first class undergraduate degree?", the answer would be "Work hard, work smart and when called for, think outside the box." Of course, there are other factors to consider and these will be addressed too. Admittedly, the task of gaining a First seems akin to climbing a mountain; but it is vital to draw your attention to this to prepare you for what's ahead. But remember mountains are conquerable for those who aspire! Understand: gaining a First Class undergraduate degree is within your grasp if you are serious about giving it your best, consistently. This is what I did, and it is only in hindsight that I came to realise I had the correct mindset and strategy to gain a First and this is the knowledge this publication will impart to you. We will also take a detailed look at how to complete all the various assessments to a high standard to get the consistent marks you need.

## 1.1  Subject scope

Strictly speaking it does not matter what degree course subject you are studying; everything said holds true for all courses. My course was a B.Eng in Computer Systems and Electronics, but that is irrelevant; the mindset and the strategy you need to gain a First in any subject is the same, as is the quality and depth of the coursework and exams.

All my coursework and some exam papers (with answers) are included as example assessments to demonstrate the level of depth and quality of answers necessary to consistently get good marks – it is not necessary to understand every explanation presented to appreciate these factors. If you present your coursework and exams to the same depth and high standard as demonstrated there is no reason why you should not achieve equal marks (many of these assessments were marked above seventy percent).

If you are studying an engineering or computer science subject there is the advantage that some examples will be meaningful to you, but that understanding is not required to appreciate what makes them of a high standard.

## 1.2  Ongoing services

As an ongoing service I would like to produce a monthly newsletter to keep you on the path to achieving a First and provide a support network website aimed at solving problems you encounter in coursework and exams revision, and providing a proof reading service. The newsletter would contain the latest degree related news and tips towards gaining a First, for example: how to get the best out of MS Office applications for producing coursework and other useful software I find. The newsletter would be published on the site. The network site would be based around

# INTRODUCTION

a system where members can post problems or requests for help with coursework assessments or exam questions, or request a document to be proof read.

As an account owner it will be your task to answer some of the posts you are able to on a regular basis, thus each member provides a service to the community. Those who provide solutions or proof read documents will at some point require similar help from the community on various occasions – thus it pays to participate, as everyone benefits. Proof reading would ideally use a shared system allowing different members to check the document in segments thus keeping the workload light and creating an efficient system. As a user of the service you would be likely to receive a number of answers to a posting, thus providing you with a number of ideas and directions to proceed in. A discussion board, messaging system and a motivational chart (where coursework marks can be entered and displayed to motivate members to aspire to a high standard) would also be provided.

If this is of interest to you please let me know by visiting the URL below and entering your email address and clicking 'Submit'. Suggestions are welcome and there will be a message window on the system should you wish to leave your thoughts or just a comment. I will keep everyone concerned apprised regarding this service.

http://www.1stacademy.net/supportnetwork.php.

This page can also be navigated to from the coursework index on the 1stAcademy website.

http://www.1stacademy.net/courseworkindex.php

All personal details transmitted as a result of this proposal and the details provided for enrolment to the service – should it become a workable solution to aid student studies – will be stored in a secure database. All details provided will not be passed on to any third party and will be stored inline with the regulations stated in the Data Protections Act of 1998.

## 1.3 How to use this publication

Before beginning it is import that you read chapter 6: Publishing Notes.

Generally speaking it is recommended that you read this book through once from start to finish. After this, use the Contents index to navigate through the book as you require tuition for each subject, like essays, assignments, projects or exams etc.

A lot of the help will come from viewing the various examples included with the publication as well as what you read here. The important 'global information' is contained in Chapter 2: Mindset for First Class Honours and Chapter 3: Strategy for First Class Honours.

Both of these are important throughout, but other than that the information is specific to whatever category of assessment you are working on at any current time.

You will find useful tuition for every category of assessment involved in your final degree grade and the relevant example URL paths are given throughout the book as you progress. The paths must be typed directly after the site address prefix: http://www.1stacademy.net or all coursework can be navigated to from the link below:

**http://www.1stacademy.net/courseworkindex.php**

Let's get started.

# 2. Mindset for First Class Honours

There is a difference between how hard you work and the standard of work you produce, and the frame of mind you will need to achieve a First – although both factors are linked to the mindset, as are other factors throughout this text. To quote Albert Jay Nock, who was both a steelworker and an Episcopal priest, "The mind is like the stomach: it is not how much you put into it that counts, but how much it digests."

There are a number of strengths in the First mindset. One such strength is not judging another person by first impressions or someone else's views. You should be able to look beyond prejudgment to what useful information that person may possess to help you obtain your goals. People maintain all kinds of prejudgments, and many are short sighted or lack understanding. Many people are too tied up in their views or 'values' and readily overlook a source of help because they fail to remain unbiased towards another person. That person may be the only source of help you run into.

Another strength is being an optimist. It's the old debate that we are asked at some point in life (usually over a beer): is the glass half empty or half full? Needless to say, it is far more positive to exhibit an optimistic view than that of a pessimist. Believe in the possible, not the impossible and always consider that the mind works best when open. This is not to say that scepticism and caution does not have their place – it's more a question of balance and being able to look at all sides of an equation.

In order to achieve a First most will need to change or grow their mindset to some degree. Graduating with a First is a success you need to create for yourself. This contrasts with the view that the majority of students will maintain after graduation: "my graduation grade is a product of how my studies played out as life happened to me throughout the last two years" or something to that effect. That may seem a little subtle at first so give it some consideration – the point is: you have to go out of your way to gain a First and this is something few students are prepared to do. It's a 'whatever it takes' mentality as apposed to 'I'll study when I find the time' or 'I'll do it when the deadline or exam date is closer' mentality. Or, to put it another way: the student that gains a First is one that shoots for the stars with the knowledge that they might land on the moon!

This is known to a few as the 'Law of Intention' whereby a person – student or otherwise – will only achieve what they set out to achieve (given that their mindset remains constant that is). So, if you aim for mediocrity that is exactly what you will achieve. How are you to achieve a First if you aim for a 2:1 (or think 'I will be pleased if I attain a 2:1')? Worse still is aiming not to fail. This is the 'play to win' mentality versus the 'play not to lose' mentality with respect to gaining a First or graduating with less. The student that graduates with a First is a 'whatever it takes' student and not any of the others mentioned that just happened to get lucky.

To graduate with a First you need the correct mindset – this is true of most things in life so if you have never given it much thought, keep it in mind from here on.

## 2.1     Enough semantics, let's be specific

### 2.1.1    Employment

Let us consider the employment market and your prospects of achieving the job you desire once you graduate. In 2004 over 10% of students achieved a First Class degree. In the same year 44.3% were awarded a 2:1 – that's close to 50%, especially when you consider statistics will fluctuate and universities continue to strive for outstanding results. With these figures in mind, it isn't surprising that many employers set their minimum requirements for degree qualified jobs at 2:1 – they are merely stipulating that they desire to employ the higher qualified half of graduates.

Don't be tempted to think 'it's OK if I don't succeed in getting a First, I'll be OK as long as I get a 2:1', as you will be doing yourself a disservice (as discussed a moment ago). You won't be ruling yourself out of the market because most employers are interested in 2:1 graduates, but you will have lost the edge that comes with having a First.

Look at it this way: if half – or some negligible number near it – have a 2:1 Batcher's degree, the only qualification capable of differentiating you from everyone else is a First (I discount a Masters or PhD as both classifications require a Batchelor's degree to begin study). Indeed, having a Masters or PhD may be desirable, but both of these become more appealing when accompanied with a First. Some employers stipulate the minimum of a First when advertising specialist vacancies and a tiny minority even demand a PhD. But the critical point to remember is a First differentiates you from a 2:1 graduate and everyone behind that. Incidentally, a graduate that has a First coupled with an intention to go into either the public sector outside of higher education or private sector has little need of a postgraduate degree, since a Master's is seldom asked for and a PhD is generally only required for specialist positions. A First, in the eyes of most employers, demonstrates an ability to gain a higher level degree. First class students are also first in line to be recruited to do a PhD.

The question of experience should not be ignored either, it is also of great importance, but the majority of students don't have much in the way of experience since they come to employment direct via the school, college or university route. Of course, this also presents a strong argument for opting for a sandwich degree – something you may wish to consider should the option be open to you. All points of view considered; a First Class undergraduate degree is the most valuable qualification, and one the majority of us will need to be competitive in the marketplace.

### 2.1.2 Treat your course seriously, it's an opportunity

Considering that you purchased this publication, it may be difficult to imagine you would do anything less than treat your course seriously – unless your parents made the purchase that is – but this needs to be said. It is also possible for the best students to lose focus, drift from good practice or become stuck in a rut.

You need to treat your course seriously and not get into bad habits – like missing lectures because other students appear to be enjoying a good time instead of attending class. I've seen many students lose focus and drop out of degree courses because they allowed disruptive students to influence them into bad habits or failed to treat their course seriously. It's a slippery slope once started and before long you've fallen too far behind. The chance of catching up seems less and less likely as time marches on. Inevitably the student takes the path of least resistance and drops out.

It is not uncommon for a small minority of students to become disruptive – this then becomes a nuisance for other members of the class. At this time you may think this won't happen to me, but students with good potential do fall into this or a similar trap – students that could have gained a First if they'd put their back into the course. Let's look at an example of what can happen when potential first class graduates lose focus.

On our undergraduate course we had two bright students that somehow allowed themselves to become unfocused; they were never disruptive. I believe these students had the potential to achieve a First, but instead somehow both lost focus and failed to apply themselves to the best of their ability. This may have been because they spent a lot of time in each others company, but there may have been other reasons. Over the course of the last year their marks began to suffer to the extent that both students had to re-sit modules the next year. This also means the modules concerned would have been capped, so this makes the likelihood of achieving a First remote.

Anyway, the point is, you have an opportunity to grow and better yourself throughout the rest of your life. A First can change the calibre of job(s) you are employed in once you graduate. We're talking a completely different career path here with a vastly better pay grade throughout. OK, so you could learn by the error of your ways and take a slightly different degree if (say) you graduated with less than a 2:1 and then gain a First, but you would still be two to three years behind in your career! You have an opportunity – one many will never have – don't blow it.

### 2.1.3 Don't focus on how big your workload is

As previously stated, the volume of work a student must keep up with on an undergraduate course is an obstacle (we will discuss how to manage this), but it is wrong to focus on how much work you have at any current time. Worrying (that is the result of focusing on the volume of work ahead) about how you will ever get it all done is not going to help. Many students find the concept of not focusing on big workloads tough, but seriously, it is pointless thinking about it once you have acknowledged what needs to be done. We all know the workload is going to be pressing, and that certain ways of coping with that are needed, but worrying will only ever be counter-productive.

The only way you will get all your work done is to get stuck into it and work hard. It is far better to try and enjoy the challenge each assessment presents. To be honest, no student really knows if they will complete it all, – at least it's hard to imagine that the end will one day be in sight – but if you try not to think about it and embrace the work you will become distracted from worries by the creative process of doing the work. The answer to this counter-productive way of thinking is simply to focus on getting work done.

## 2.1.4 Building confidence

You should be confident about your ability to get good marks for the work you submit. Being confident about getting good marks will help you when producing an assessment. For example: if you are confident of getting a good grade with an assignment for a specific subject, you are likely to produce the work to greater standard of depth and quality.

Imagine working on an assignment with the thought 'I hope I manage to get more than fifty percent this time' echoing in your mind. Do you think you will produce good work? You will probably produce an assignment worth fifty to sixty percent but you won't produce the consistently high marks needed to gain a First. This kind of thinking can develop with students who get passable to average marks with coursework and exams in the first and second year. Since the first year doesn't count towards graduation and the second year is typically factored to thirty percent, it is still possible to gain a First. It is possible to turn it around, but some things are going to need to change!

So, if you have developed such a 'negative' thought process, you need to replace it with a 'positive' one. This is going to be a conscious effort on your part as negative thoughts don't go away easily, but by correcting your mind when you catch yourself being less than confident, with a counter thought that is positive in nature, you can adjust confidence over time. This will be reflected to some degree in your marks. Believe that the day will come where you get near to seventy percent or maybe a little more and build on that so that your confidence continues to increase.

So what thought should you replace such negativity with? Try something to the effect of 'my marks are proportion to the effort I apply, this time I will do more research and work harder', or something to that description. Having this publication and applying the knowledge contained within when producing your next assessment will also help build your confidence, so continue reading and begin to make the appropriate changes.

## 2.1.5 Collaboration

It's a good idea to collaborate with your fellow students in an effort to get work done, or find out how to do something you don't fully understand. For one thing, you don't always get chance in every lecture to ask the lecturer for a recap of what you've just been shown. Also, students in your class may be able to explain whatever it is in a different way to the lecturer – a way that you find it easier to understand. Actually, some lecturers are not as good as one would hope when it comes to explaining certain subjects or techniques, or even just imparting a lecture itself. It's often useful to have something explained differently – to get a different take on whatever it is.

It can prove helpful to work with another student on an essay or assignments too, providing the work you hand in is clearly distinguishable as your own. It is amazing how much time can be saved by working with another student: two students studying together often succeed in understanding a problem in less time than one studying alone. This puts both students in a position to progress on their own. Generally when two students work together in this way, both will benefit from the joint effort. Two students with a less than complete understanding of a subject will understand different aspects of the subject, and thus one quickly learns from the other. Also, remember not to discount a student from being useful for some reason, you might be pleasantly surprised with the direction gained by having a new member in your study group.

### 2.1.6 Maintain a good relationship with your lecturers

You should always do your best to maintain a good relationship with your lecturers, and given that you are a good student, it is not difficult to do so. We are not discussing being a so called 'teacher's pet' here – just being friendly and not taking advantage or doing something that may tick them off. Continually doing something like that can put them offside.

You need them to feel inclined to give you the benefit of the doubt should something unforeseen arise. When you need their help – with (for example) an extended hand in date for an assignment – you don't want them refusing your request because you have done something silly once too often. Always show them respect and gratitude when they help you. Remember, they don't have to help you in such cases, but it's useful when they do and chances are you will need to ask them for the odd extension.

### 2.1.7 Motivation

To produce good work you need to be motivated. It is easier to do any task well when we are motivated to do it. It is also easier to be motivated when we enjoy doing what ever it is. Motivation is the force that drives us to produce good work – so if you are to get a First you will need a bucket load of it.

The best way to maintain motivation is to choose a degree you will enjoy. If you have already embarked on your course and are finding motivation a problem then you may want to consider if you are on the right course. Should you find a more suitable course, ask if it is possible to switch without having to lose any time. In some circumstances – if it has not been left too long – it is possible to catch up by obtaining notes and handouts from the lectures missed and putting in some extra time at home.

Motivation can also dwindle if you mix with students that are easily distracted and allow them to draw you into bad habits and practices. This has been discussed previously, so if motivation is lacking, consider whether this could be the problem. If so, the path to redeeming your motivation needs to begin with distancing yourself from such students in your class or university and finding yourself a more dedicated group to associate with.

Motivation is like confidence in that it can be boosted. Anytime you catch yourself feeling apathetic you need to stop yourself and replace the thoughts you are thinking with a positive, motivation-provoking thought. It can be as simple as one of the below.

*I will stay motivated and work towards getting a First.*
*I am motivated, gaining a First will ensure I get the job I want.*
*I enjoy working towards my goals of graduating with First Class honours.*

These thoughts are also classed as affirmations, which when used regularly, can have a positive outcome. Affirmations are known to be helpful with building motivation and confidence as well as a host of other things. Why not Google 'affirmations' and find out more.

Should you want to see what degree courses are available to choose from, use the link below.

**http://www.ucas.ac.uk/students/choosingcourses/choosingcourse/ chooserightcourse**

## 2.1.8 Sickness or other unavoidable interruptions

If you have to miss an exam or a hand in date due to being ill, or some other unforeseen, unavoidable 'serious' event you must give your lecturer(s) a full explanation, specifically if it's illness. Some people are uncomfortable talking about certain illnesses or conditions, but it is vital to do this as it can be the difference between sitting a 40% capped re-sit or being able to collect full marks on a re-sit paper.

I was unable to sit two exams at the end of the second year due to illness, but because I provided a full explanation I sat both exams two months later and kept all my marks while others around me were capped at 40%. The papers were re-sit papers, but the fullness of my explanation made me exempt from mark capping. I also had the whole summer to revise and sailed through both papers. Later I was told that even though I'd explained the mitigating circumstances I was lucky – apparently it is rare that any student sits a re-sit paper and is allowed to keep full marks. So if you miss an exam due to illness you may still get capped in a re-sit, those who say nothing or give a weak explanation will certainly have to be content with 40%.

## 2.2 Getting the balance right

It is important to strike a balance between working towards your degree and time out, and the other facets of your life. It is not productive to work yourself past the point when you have really had enough and need a rest, so much so that the quality of your work decreases. You need to know how long you can work in a session without your work beginning to deteriorate because you have been pushing yourself too far – and this is different for everyone. Also be wary that working too late in the evening can affect quality of sleep, and thus you will not be at your best the next day and again, your work will suffer.

Another important thing is not to put working to earn money in a part time job before your degree in terms of importance. We all like to earn money and subsidize our student lifestyle, but ultimately your degree is of more importance. A degree is something that most people only study for once in a lifetime, and your graduation grade has a direct bearing on your ability to attract the postgraduate job of choice. Bottom line: if your job is adversely affecting studying for your degree because you don't have enough time to study, then it is best to reduce your hours or find a job with fewer hours.

Most part time employers that employ students should be understanding if you inform them that you simply need more time for studying and ask for a reduction in hours.

Worst case scenario, you could quit the job and find another part time job at the end of the academic year. Some students do put a job before their degree and unfortunately in my experience it has always been a tale of woe. Part time work is easy to come by – there is no shortage of it. And, you can always get a 'stand in' job after you finish your degree and are seeking employment in your chosen field.

# 3. Strategy for First Class Honours

By far the biggest problem you face when studying for a degree is the volume of work you will have at any one time, specifically in the last semester of the second and third year as your coursework will be coupled with exam revision. The toughest time, when your workload is at its worst, is the last term of the third year, but ideally, you need to be prepared with the correct strategy for the start of the second year. Remember, the first year has no bearing on your final grade. For example, when I studied for my degree, in the last term of the third year my workload was four assignments, a major project presentation and report (or dissertation as it is often called) as well as three exams to revise for.

Happily, one subject was completely assignment-based, but whilst that was an upside, the downside was that we had one more assignment to stand in the way of revision for the remaining three exams. It was a tense couple of months, with little time for anything other than studies of one mode or another. So what strategy do you need to gain a First, given the ongoing workload you will experience throughout the final two years?

The main facets in the strategy you require are as follows: treat each assessment in your workload with equal importance. Work hard, work smart, multitask and when called for, think outside the box. There are other facets to consider too, but we'll deal with them after the first five.

## 3.1 Treat each assessment in your workload with equal importance.

You need to treat each assessment in your workload with equal importance. This is very important, as are all facets in this strategy, but many students without a strategy for getting a good grade with fall into an inherent trap here. Each assessment you have to complete in your degree carries a different number of points – that is, some assessments have a higher weighting than others. For example, in one subject you may have three assignments and an exam. In another subject it is highly likely that you will have only one assignment and one exam. Clearly, the separate assessments in the first subject have a lower weighting towards your final grade than those in the second. The assessments in the second subject carry greater weighting than those in the first, and in reality, in all degrees, there are a number of assessments that carry small, or even very small weightings.

Because some assessments carry a low mark, or weighting, some students will prioritise essays, assignments, etc. Worse still, they will not treat lower weighted assessments seriously and concentrate only on the assessments that carry a high weighing. Not treating all assessments with equal importance or prioritising high weighted assessments over low weighted assessments is a perilous path if you desire a First.

On the surface, when faced with a number of assessments to complete within the same timeframe, prioritising may seem like a good strategy – but things are not always what they seem. The problem is the overall mark you require to gain a First weighed against the weighting factor of each assessment. That is, you are not going to score highly on every assessment you complete; some assessments may only yield average marks. Let's discuss a hypothetical example to demonstrate why this is an important facet to the overall strategy: A student has five subjects in his final year meeting the marking criteria in Table 1 – assume his second year mark was 70% and that the contribution weighting of the second year is 30% (a typical percentage).

|  | – Assessments – | | | | |
|---|---|---|---|---|---|
| Subject 1 | Assignment 1 = 20% | Assignment 2 = 20% | Assignment 3 = 20% | Assignment 4 = 20% | Exam = 20% |
| Mark: | 68% | 69% | 65% | 69% | 50% |
| Subject 2 | Assignment = 40% | Essay = 20% | Exam = 40% | – | – |
| Mark: | 68% | 41% | 51% | – | – |
| Subject 3 | Assignment 1 = 20% | Assignment 2 = 40% | Exam = 40% | – | – |
| Mark: | 44% | 67% | 79% | – | – |
| Subject 4 | Assignment 1 = 50% | Exam = 50% | – | – | – |
| Mark: | 70% | 69% | – | – | – |
| Project | Report = 70% | Viva = 30% | – | – | – |
| Mark: | 71% | 59% | – | – | – |
| Year 2 | Value = 30% | | | | |
| Mark: | 70% | | | | |

Table 1. Why all assessments should be treated with equal importance part 1.

Below is a set of calculations to workout the student's overall graduation grade – the method an examination board uses may differ from this, but it is close enough to demonstrate the significance.

$$Subject1 = \frac{20 \times 68}{100} + \frac{20 \times 69}{100} + \frac{20 \times 65}{100} + \frac{20 \times 69}{100} + \frac{20 \times 50}{100} = 64\%$$

$$Subject2 = \frac{40 \times 68}{100} + \frac{20 \times 41}{100} + \frac{40 \times 51}{100} = 55.8\%$$

$$Subject3 = \frac{20 \times 44}{100} + \frac{40 \times 67}{100} + \frac{40 \times 79}{100} = 67.2\%$$

$$Subject4 = \frac{50 \times 70}{100} + \frac{50 \times 69}{100} = 69.5\%$$

$$project = \frac{70 \times 71}{100} + \frac{30 \times 69}{100} = 67.4\%$$

$$Secondyear = \frac{30 \times 70}{100} = 21\%$$

$$OverallGrade = \frac{64 + 55.8 + 67.2 + 69.5 + 67.4 + 21}{5} = 68.98\%$$

Our student has narrowly missed a First and achieved a 2:1 given that the mark to gain a 2:1 is 60% or above. Let's take a more critical look at this example. The student's mark for the essay of subject two was significantly below the other assessment marks, the same is true of assignment one of subject three, and the rest of the marks are respectable.

The student may have regarded the two assessments in question to be of lesser importance as they carry a lower weighting than others (each only being worth 20%). Let's assume to gain a First the student requires 70% or greater and let's bump the two weak assessments up to 75% and 73% respectively and recalculate the grand total (table overleaf):

| Subject 1 | Assignment 1 = 20% | Assignment 2 = 20% | – Assessments –<br>Assignment 3 = 20% | Assignment 4 = 20% | Exam = 20% |
|---|---|---|---|---|---|
| Mark: | 68% | 69% | 65% | 69% | 50% |
| Subject 2 | Assignment = 40% | Essay = 20% | Exam = 40% | – | – |
| Mark: | 68% | 75% | 51% | – | – |
| Subject 3 | Assignment 1 = 20% | Assignment 2 = 40% | Exam = 40% | – | – |
| Mark: | 73% | 67% | 79% | – | – |
| Subject 4 | Assignment 1 = 50% | Exam = 50% | – | – | – |
| Mark: | 70% | 69% | – | – | – |
| Project | Report = 70% | Viva = 30% | – | – | – |
| Mark: | 71% | 59% | – | – | – |
| Year 2 | Value = 30% | | | | |
| Mark: | 70% | | | | |

**Table 2. Why all assessments should be treated with equal importance part 2.**

$$Subject1 = \frac{20 \times 68}{100} + \frac{20 \times 69}{100} + \frac{20 \times 65}{100} + \frac{20 \times 69}{100} + \frac{20 \times 50}{100} = 64\%$$

$$Subject2 = \frac{40 \times 68}{100} + \frac{20 \times 75}{100} + \frac{40 \times 51}{100} = 62.6\%$$

$$Subject3 = \frac{20 \times 73}{100} + \frac{40 \times 67}{100} + \frac{40 \times 79}{100} = 73\%$$

$$Subject4 = \frac{50 \times 70}{100} + \frac{50 \times 69}{100} = 69.5\%$$

$$project = \frac{70 \times 71}{100} + \frac{30 \times 69}{100} = 67.4\%$$

$$Second year = \frac{30 \times 70}{100} = 21\%$$

$$OverallGrade = \frac{64 + 62.6 + 73 + 69.5 + 67.4 + 21}{5} = 71.5\%$$

As seen, our student has now achieved a First. It can be clearly seen that prioritising is an incorrect facet to adopt in a strategy to gain a First, and treating all assessments with equal importance is vital. However, as with many things, there is an exception to the rule.

### 3.1.1 The exception to the rule

As mentioned, there is an exception to the rule with this facet of the strategy, but it must only be used as a last resort. The exception is when you are overloaded with a number of assessments that need to be completed simultaneously, and it is obvious that some deadlines cannot be met. In a worst case scenario you can improvise by prioritising based on the weighting of each assessment. Let's be clear about the worst case scenario; before you consider improvising the strategy you must always consider what you may be able to do to avoid it. In such a situation, and this is very likely to occur by the way, you should appeal to the lecturer of each subject for which you have simultaneous assessments and ask if the hand in dates can be rescheduled so that you are able to give each assessment the time and attention it merits.

Most lecturers will be accommodating and will move a hand in date by a week or so for the whole class – this is your first play and it is suggested you ask the lecturers concerned when you are in the company of fellow students. It is easier to say no to a single person, but not so easy when you have company. You are only likely to be declined if a lecturer has good reason, which is only likely to happen at the end of the third semester. In such a last resort, find the assessment with the lowest weighting and do as best as you can with it, but give the higher weighted assessments greater priority. Never skip an assessment, thinking it's only worth ten or twenty percent; for one thing the lecturer concerned will not be impressed and as said you need them onside. Always do the best you can with those low weighed assessments in whatever little time you can afford them.

## 3.2   Work hard: work smart

Most – if not all – students embarking on a degree are not prepared for the outsized workload they have let themselves in for: worse still, many put their brain in neutral and party whilst having coursework to complete. Staying on top of your workload is vital to the strategy. If you have an assignment that doesn't have to be in for four weeks, you should be working on it – maybe at a moderate pace as it is only one assignment, but it must be a work in progress until you judge it finished.

There are too may students who get coursework a month or so before the hand in date and mistakenly think they have time to burn. Don't take my word for it and then gravitate back to undisciplined practices over a semester or two – there are a number of reasons why this is poor management of your *overall* workload:

- Good students use their time constructively – foolish students squander time on frivolities. Once your assignment is finished or during completing it, you have plenty of time to make sure you understand every aspect of your lectures. Understanding lectures in entirety is vital. There are three reasons: A) Over time you will forget details. If you fully understand every concept imparted, or lecture as a whole, it will make the revision process easier when it comes. Therefore you will be better prepared for exams. B) You may get an aspect of a lecture you don't understand and need time to research it at home – not easy if you have left your one assignment to the last moment. C) You simply need to know your stuff – not just now, but throughout your career.
- You may get more coursework and suddenly find you have two or three assessments of one nature or another. You usually have an idea of when to expect assessments as good lecturers keep you informed, but remember that the unexpected can occur from time to time. It's all about being prepared again.
- Student debt – if you are staying in doing your work you are not out spending your student loan. One way or another life keeps your nose to the grindstone after graduation (nothing really changes then), so it's not good to spend the whole loan and borrow large sums of money elsewhere at an inflated rate. Think overtime to pay off debt – or make ends meet – not time-out with your future spouse or friends.
- Things aren't always what they seem. You think you're in the clear with time on your hands and only one assignment to complete in a month, but in the last three or four days you reach an aspect of your assignment you don't understand or have overlooked. It amounts to something you have failed to take into consideration, with time in short supply you're unable to work it out and finish every aspect. Thus you lose marks that better planning would have prevented.

Another aspect of working hard – the topic we just discussed is biased towards working smart – is that of doing every item justice; be thorough. By being thorough you ensure a good mark and good marks ensure your First Class degree. You have my coursework – you only need to look through it to see how thorough it is. Always try to do everything asked of you in your assessment brief and, if you can, throw a thing or two extra in for good measure. It is likely that from time to time, you will misinterpret something in an assignment or your project dissertation and, consequently lose a few marks. Worse still, you may get something wrong or may not be able to get something working and end up losing considerable marks. Putting something extra in, going that extra mile as it were, can claw some lost marks back; reclaiming those marks (or getting a few extra for going out of your way) may tip the scales in your favour when graduating.

This next point is something that mainly applies to engineering degrees or a few other areas that escape my mind. It is always more impressive when a student gets (say) the device at the centre of their project working. It's very gratifying for the student too. But this can be tricky, especially in areas like software or electronics – it can take a lot of time and unrevealing of what you failed to anticipate or overlooked. I succeeded in getting most, if not all, software programs or circuits to work that were requested to work. As the project subject was cited for this discussion, let's examine it more closely.

A typical major project in the final year of your degree may comprise of the following marking criteria: background 15%, competence 15%, achievement 30%, viva and report 30%. Getting the project to work will reflect on competence and achievement. Instantly, you have (say) approximately 10 – 15 percent to add to the overall mark. That will certainly help you in the desired direction. It's worth working hard (or smart) to make sure you have enough time to go around and get things working as apposed to presenting a work in progress or something that didn't quite workout. By the way, my HNC project didn't quite work out, the verdict was that it was over ambitious, but I still worked hard enough to get a distinction. It goes to show the effort is worthwhile.

Getting things to work usually takes more than a little passion. If you are passionate about your course (or most of it as it is difficult to be passionate about every subject) that will also be a big factor in helping you gain a First.

Another reason you need to work hard is your ability to even out the areas of your course that you have weakness in – there will be weak areas in your arsenal unless you are exceptionally clever. You do not have to be exceptionally clever to get a First, and the 'exceptionally' implies these students are in the minority. Indeed they are; there are two kinds of people capable of getting a First, those who are exceptionally clever and those who work hard and have a good strategy. Extraordinary results can be achieved when you work hard without being exceptionally clever. Incidentally, plenty of exceptionally cleaver students mismanage their workload and end up graduating with something less than a First. It happens all the time.

So, if you are like most, you may have the odd weaknesses in your arsenal, topics where you have to work extra hard or put in more time to study to grasp a technique, concept or to understand something in its entirety. Whatever it is it makes no difference: if you put your mind to it and give it enough attention you will accomplish an understanding. It all comes back to staying on top of your workload so as to allow extra time to balance out those weaker areas, so when exams finally come and you're separated from your notes you are still able to produce a respectable mark.

Always remember you may have an exam or assignment where you get little more than a pass. The more you can strengthen a weak area and squeeze through some extra marks the more likely it is that you will get a First. In such cases, every mark scored counts because the panel grading your work has to draw a line somewhere and you want to end up on the right side. One or two marks in an assessment may be the difference between an Upper Second and a First. Giving an area you are weak in some extra attention can make a world of difference.

Working hard and smart is very important, it cannot be stressed enough. At times, it is the only facet in the strategy that will get you through. On the subject of working smart we need to discuss another First saving facet – it's a vital one too.

## 3.3 Multitask

You are going to have simultaneous coursework, that is, several assessments to work on at one time. Like any good computer operating system, you need to multitask. There are two methods for working on multiple assessments that work very well – we'll begin with my favourite, and probably the most practical considering the nature of the work it is being applied too.

Begin work by taking one item (say) an assignment or your project dissertation and work on it until you get stuck and are unable to progress further. Never worry about getting stuck – it is an opportunity to put one item down and begin working on another – and the answer for the aspect you are stuck with will come when you have the opportunity to research it further with your lecturer or another student. It may also simply be something someone else says that sets you thinking in a new direction, causing you to overcome said problem.

Have you ever watched 'House' or 'House MD' as it is known in the United States? House often gets stuck and cannot solve his current medical case – he is a diagnostic doctor who will only accept cases that 'interest' him, cases that other doctors are unable to solve. Then someone says something to him in conversation, like his pal Wilson or boss Cuddy, and suddenly his mind begins to think in a different direction, and before long he solves the case. While you are stuck on your current assessment you can't move forward, so don't keep trying; put it aside and begin working on another assessment. Work on that assessment until you get stuck again or have the solution to the item you have put aside.

Say you get stuck a second time without a solution arising for the first assessment, put that assessment aside and begin or continue working on item three, then on assessment four, and so on. Let's look at the second method.

In method two you simply work on one item until you find a convenient place to stop and then begin or continue to work on a second or third assessment, and so on. It doesn't really matter how you multitask so long as you do so effectively. It's whatever works best for you. Some students may find the second method takes more discipline as you have to interrupt your flow of thought at the so-called convenient point and pick up another item and continue with it. The best action is to use both methods dependant on circumstances.

## 3.4  Thinking outside the box

This is important. You are going to be asked to solve some difficult problems (assessments) – often more than one at a time – so being able to think outside the box is a desirable asset. Teaching someone to do this is difficult, so an example of my own will have to suffice to start you thinking of different ways an assessment could be solved (or written), providing you with the key to completing it.

Remember I referred to an Object Orientated Programming (OOP) assignment that resulted in over half the class dropping out? I thought outside the box to solve this one and in the end it was the only reason I was able to complete the assignment with a 100% working computer program and gain around 80% in the assignment.

We were asked to solve a routing problem, or more accurately put, to write a computer program to find either the shortest or the cheapest routes from one node to another node over a multi-node computer network. The program was to be object orientated and written in C++. The problem was twofold to my reckoning. First, it was a complex problem that required a recursive algorithm to explore all possible routes around the network and second, we were being asked to write the program in object orientated C++, a language none of us were particularly fluent in. We'd only been programming it for one term! The program also had to be capable of solving any network loaded from a file on a disk.

Imagine being asked to explain a complex problem in German when your native language is English and your German is limited to reduced vocabulary. Surely it would be easier to explore said problem in English and then translate the solution into German? This makes a lot of sense – the overall task is broken into two steps (or byte size pieces) allowing you to tackle them individually instead of together. Stepping away from the analogy, back to the computer program, arriving at the mechanics of the solution would be only half as difficult if it were to be written in another language the programmer was fully versed in. He or she would be able to get it completely working before thinking about translating it into another language.

Fortunately programming in Visual Basic (VB) was an existing skill of mine, so I wrote a program that solved the routing problem in VB. Even in VB, coding a recursive algorithm to solve the routing problem was difficult. It took two attempts, the first being ditched in favour of starting over. After finishing the second VB program it worked 100% and solved any network I created as a loadable file. More importantly, my solution satisfied all the criteria set forth in the assignment brief – except one, it wasn't written in OOP C++.

It took considerable time to translate into OOP C++; it didn't help that the computer crashed every time the program was executed. It proved fortunate that the approach of programming two programs had been adopted as I was able to single step both side by side, the C++ version in the MS debugger and the VB version in the VB debugger. Many bugs were found in the C++ version by comparing variable values, strings and jumps etc. Without a comparison to test the C++ version alongside it would never have been completed. In the end it worked perfectly.

I am not sure how this will equate to you thinking outside the box to solve or write an assessment, but specifically, you need to be asking yourself how else could an assessment brief be accomplished that isn't being advertised in said brief. How can the task be broken into smaller, bite size pieces making it easier to arrive at an overall solution? What techniques do you already possess that can find a solution even when it isn't the solution being asked for? These (and others) are the questions you need to ask yourself should you find yourself cursing the lecturer after leaving the classroom with the latest addition to your workload.

## 3.5   When is an item finished?

This can be a little tricky in some cases. With some assessments – programming a computer program is a good example – it is often easy to see improvements or new features to add that may (or may not) produce more marks. But with a degree, because of the sizeable workload, it is important to be able to recognise when you've done enough to get a good grade for the assessment in question. To clarify, you should aim to get a First on every item worked on and as said, to ensure this throw a little something extra in if you can.

In finite terms, an assessment, whether it is an essay, assignment or project report is finished when you have met all aspects of the brief or specification – in short, when you have been thorough and done everything asked for. If you can see something that can be added on the off chance of gaining a few extra marks then do so providing it isn't going to take long. The reason computer programs are a good example is it's often possible to add features by simply including options in the human interface to invoke functions directly that are normally only executed as part of the overall program. By doing so you get extra functions (which is generally impressively received by the lecturer) without doing extra work.

# 4. Coursework

## 4.1 Backing up and saving work regularly

Always keep a backup of your work on a separate medium; a USB drive or a second networked computer are excellent options. Also, and this is vital, continuously save your work every five minutes or so. Don't be tempted to think this is excessive or bordering on paranoia, it is better to be a 'perpetual saver' than lose work through something unforeseen. These days computers and operating systems are very reliable but there was a day when this was not so. Even so, with all the improvements afforded them, computers sometimes do something unexpected resulting in loss of work. Remember, saving your work is only ever a mouse click away!

Backing up work is vital. Many Internet Service Providers (ISPs) now offer backup services with their connection – this is another suggested option. Also, some antivirus programs like Norton 360 offer backup services too. Never only keep one copy of your work, the loss of several items of work is almost certainly liable to wreck your degree.

## 4.2 How to present your coursework

Your coursework should always be presented accurate to the brief you are given by your lecturer – always make sure you are clear on exactly what they expect for each assessment. You should present your subject headings in the Harvard style (as used in this book). Microsoft Word makes it easy to do this, so it is suggested you stick with the Microsoft Office software. In the MS Office suite there are a number of programs that will be useful throughout your degree. Alternatively, Sun produces an open source alternative to MS Office, it is called Open Office and it is very good, but not as powerful or flexible as the Microsoft products (Google will easily find this for you). I'm going to assume you will use MS Office as I know most of you will.

You should use the following programs for the following tasks:

- Word – All written assessments.
- Excel – this is useful for producing any spreadsheets you may need. It can often make quick work of mathematical tasks where a number of alternate variables need to be considered in complex equations.
- Power Point – use this program to produce any OHP slides you need, e.g. for your project presentations.
- Project – Use this to produce Gant charts for your project reports.
- Visio – is useful for producing flowcharts or flow diagrams and Unified Modelling Language (UML) style diagrams.

All work created in MS Office applications can be used with Word to produce your assessments by inserting the item into your Word documents where appropriate.

Other programs you may find of use:

- Paint Shop Pro – excellent for drawing. The browse feature is practically useful as it will show you a miniature of all the pictures in each directory. Adobe Photoshop is also very popular and comparable to PSP.
- Microsoft Visual Studios (which includes Visual C++, Visual Basic, Visual C#, Visual J++, Visual J# (both are Java variants), and others if you are studying engineering or computer science subjects.
- MatLab by MathWorks, again if you are studying engineering or computer science subjects.

In a moment we will save some time by discussing how to set up MS Word font styles (Sun Open Office is very similar). This will allow you to insert a Harvard style contents index easily. Incidentally, not all of my assignments use a Harvard style index as this is something I didn't wise up to until somewhere in the third year.

Another presentation style you should be aware of when writing assessments is to write them in the third person, avoiding using words like: I, my and me etc. Essays may differ with regard to this practice so check with your lecturer, but we'll take a detailed look at essays later.

Again, not all of my reports are written in the third person, but generally speaking, those produced in the third year are. Some students find it difficult to write in the third person continually throughout an assessment at first, but don't fret about this, it will come given practice. Also, steer away from using contractions (like isn't, can't, you'll etc.) as academic publications tend to avoid them.

### 4.2.1 General Coursework assessment tips

Here are nine tips that are relevant to essays, assignments and report writing:

1. Pay attention to the format and presentation of your coursework. Be careful not to lose marks through poor spelling or use of grammar, improper margins and other errors that are easily avoided. Familiarise yourself with all coursework writing requirements by asking your lecturer. Use a word processor and spell and grammar check your work throughout.

2. Write concisely and clearly – this forces you to think clearly. Since language is a tool to express thought, sloppy use of language implies sloppy thinking. Avoid passive sentences; try to use verbs correctly to write active sentences. Communicate ideas and arguments in a consistent tone and always check definitions of words that you are unsure of. Once you have completed a draft copy review your work, remove superfluous words, and tweak the language to make sure it flows throughout.

3. When reviewing language consider the structure of paragraphs and how they may be reorganised to improve flow and tone. A sharp flowing delivery of the material you present will always carry greater impact. Explore the use of different words by using the thesaurus tool when you are unsure if you have chosen the best language – this often improves on first choice.

4. Cut and paste is a powerful tool for restructuring, but be sure to reintegrate the text accurately as this invariably leads to the need to the change suffixes of nouns and adjectives. After any reconstructing and tweaking also consider whether your introduction is setting up the

subject and the content to full effect and the conclusion clearly summarises the main arguments.

5. Never plagiarise. Do not copy other people's work in any way – always use the proper citations when researching a subject from existing sources. Do not take someone else's work and change words around, it is still considered to be cheating. In extreme cases students caught plagiarising have been expelled and banned from returning to higher education. Also remember that there is computer software that is able to identify plagiarism which is used in the submission process. Also remember, researched work with the proper citations in footnotes and reference sections is actually favoured by lecturers and increases marks.

6. If your understanding is less than complete when approaching any assessment or subject, look for examples. When clarification is needed regarding the format of a specific assessment, be it an essay, assignment or project report etc., then there are a wealth of examples included with this publication to guide you. If you need clarification on how to present a specific topic research it and observe how the author(s) introduce the topic, develop ideas and provides a clear conclusion. You may also want to look at similar topics to be sure you are writing to standards associated with the relevant field.

7. Organisation of researched material is critical when writing any item, not only do you have to read the material, you have to clearly organise the information you are presenting – see 4.2.4.2 Structure and 4.2.4.3 Body, although these are specifically relevant to writing compelling essays they are also methods you can use on assignments and project reports where required.

8. It is important to clearly understand any subject you are required to base an assessment on. You might want to underline key words in the research gathered and think about how they relate to the readers and/or lectures. If in doubt, always ask your lecturer or other students for clarification.

9. Start early and budget your time, as outlined in 3.2 Work hard: work smart.

### 4.2.2 Making the most of feedback

Once you have produced an item of coursework (typically essays and assignments) and handed it in for marking it is important to put the feedback from your lecturer to good use. Most – if not all – faculties will provide a marking assessment sheet after your current item of coursework has been marked; this will include a feedback section. The comments lecturers leave as feedback can often provide useful information that can be used to improve your future coursework assessments. So, as you start each new assessment, take a look at your last marking assessment sheet, read the feedback comments and see if there is something or a number of things that you can improve on this time round. Alternatively, you may like to keep a record (say) in your diary of a number of points to improve in future work gathered from feedback given in marking assessments that you can use to remind yourself before starting your next assessment.

### 4.2.3 Setting up font styles

This should save you time as styles can be a little tricky to setup. Start up Word and select Format/Styles and Formatting from the menu. When you begin with a fresh document your style menu will look something like Figure 1. (Throughout this section American spellings are used in figures and tables to reflect accuracy with regard to controls in MS Word.)

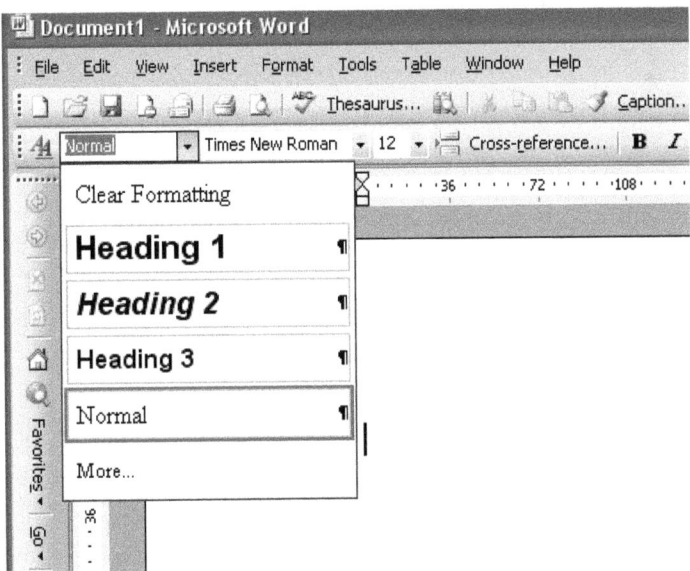

**Figure 1. How your style menu will look with a new document.**

When finished your styles menu will look something like the one below, Figure 2.

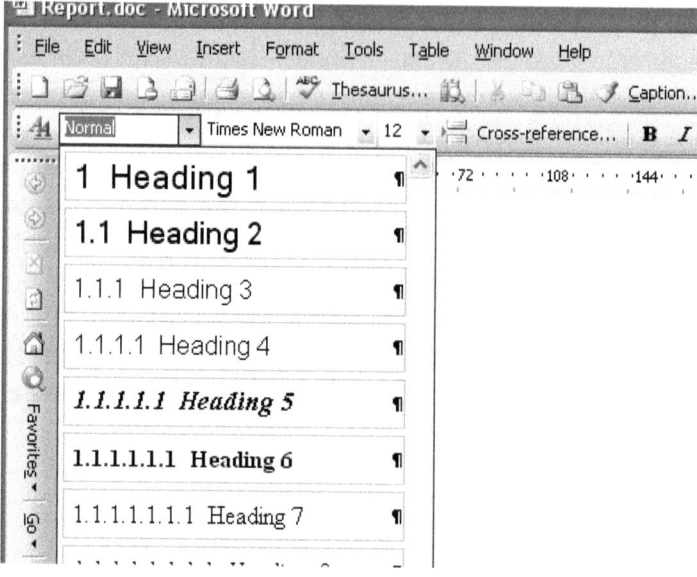

Figure 2. How your style menu should look for assessments.

Click on Heading 1 in the right hand Style and Formatting panel, right click and select Modify from the cursor menu. In the window that appears, click on Format and select Font. The font window will open; see Figure 3.

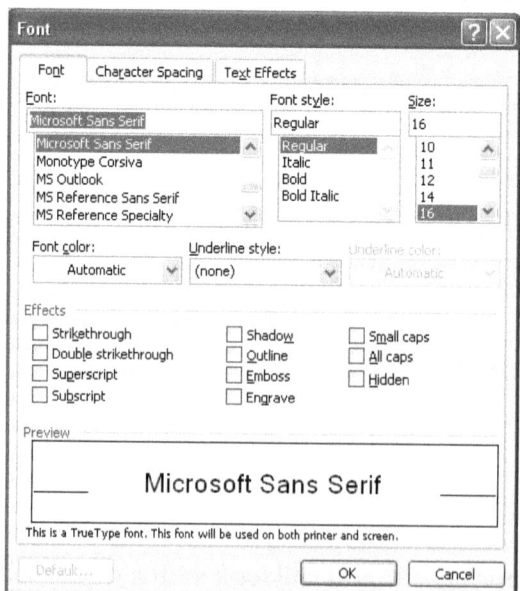

Figure 3. The font window showing the settings for heading 1.

For headings you will want to use Microsoft Sans Serif, so scroll through and select this under Font. Next select Regular in Font style. Now select 16 in Size. Font color should be Automatic and Underline style is (none). None of the Effects should be checked. Now click OK and select Paragraph from the Format button. The window in Figure 4 will appear.

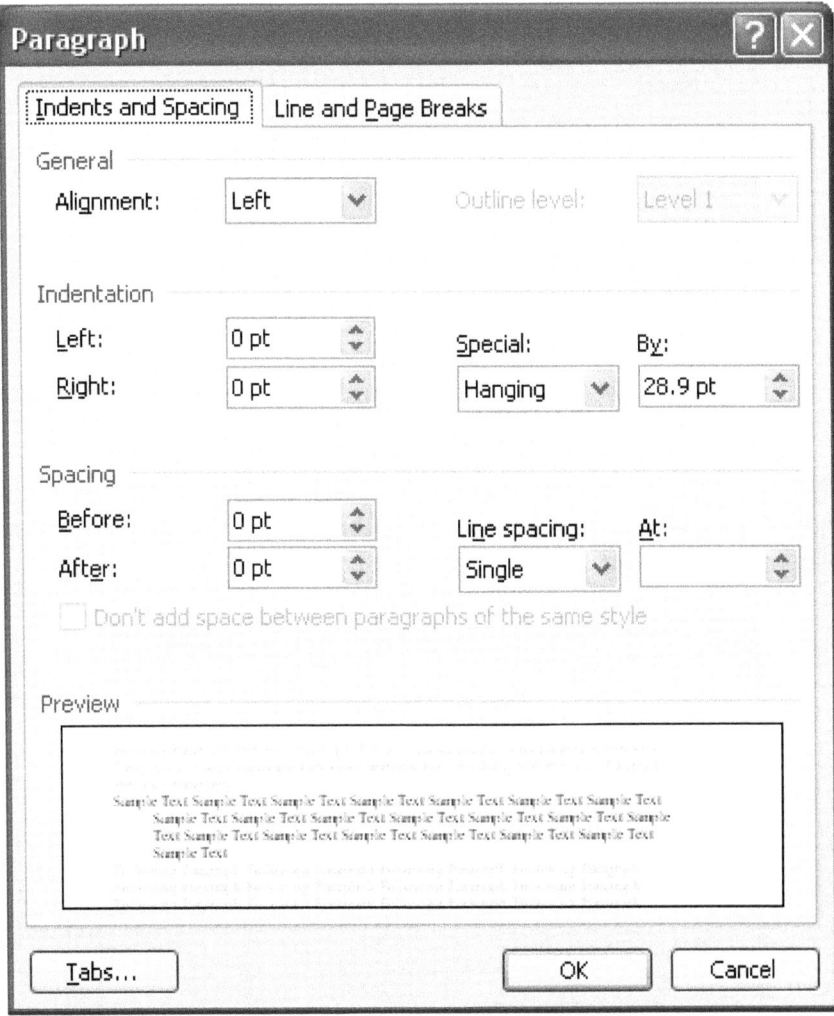

Figure 4. The paragraph window showing the setup for heading 1.

Now, for Heading 1 you need to change the items as follows (some of them will already be set correct). General Alignment = Left, Indentation Left = 0, Right = 0, Special = Hanging, By = 28.9, Spacing Before = 0, After = 0, Line spacing = Single, At = empty. Now click OK and select Tabs from the Format button. The window in Figure 5 will appear (overleaf).

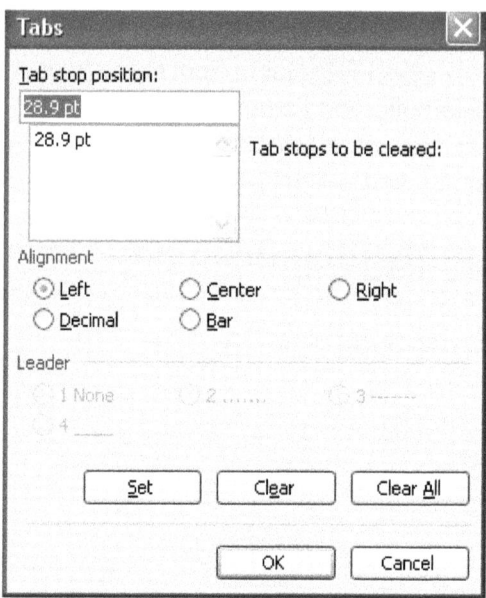

Figure 5. The Tabs window showing the settings for Heading 1.

Now change the Tab stop position to 28.9pt. The Alignment needs to be set to Left. Click OK and select Numbering from the Format button. The window in Figure 6 will appear.

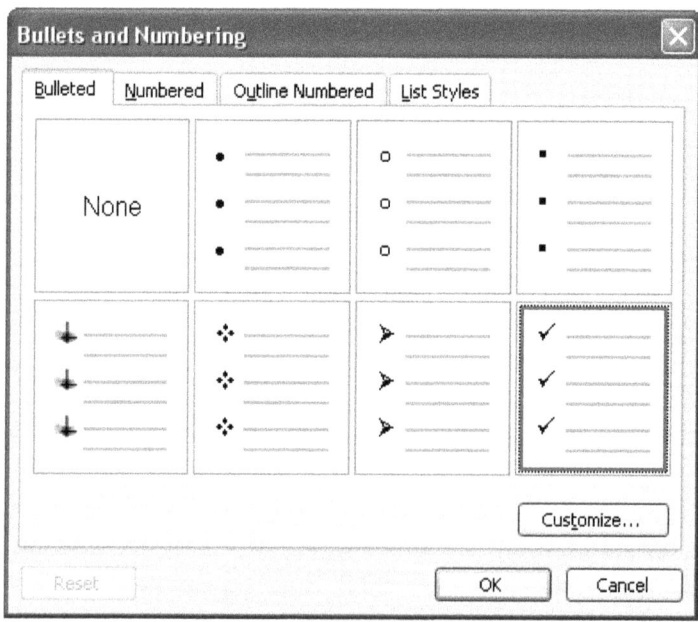

Figure 6. The Bulleted setting for Heading 1.

On the Bulleted tab select the bottom right square. Now click on the Numbered tab.

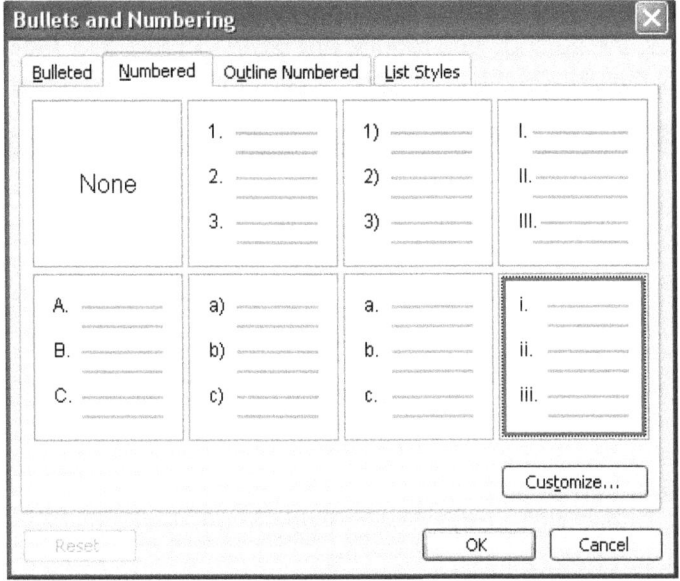

Figure 7. The Numbered setting for Heading 1.

On the Numbered tab select the bottom right square. Now click on the Outline Numbered tab.

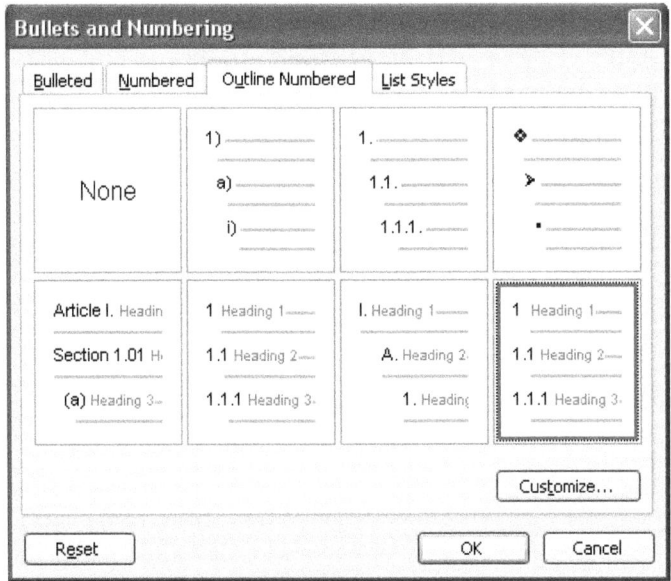

Figure 8. The Outline Numbered setting for Heading 1.

Finally, on the Outline Numbered tab, Figure 8, select the bottom right square. Now click OK. Click OK again on the Modify Style window. You have now set up the Heading 1 style. You now need to repeat this process for a few more styles; the settings you require are given in Table 3 to Table 6. Don't forget to select the style in the right hand Style and Formatting panel.

| Heading 2 ||
|---|---|
| **Font** ||
| Font | Microsoft Sans Serif |
| Font style | Regular |
| Size | 14 |
| **Paragraph** ||
| General Alignment | Left |
| Outline level | Level 2 |
| Indentation Left | 0 |
| Indentation Right | 0 |
| Indentation Special | Hanging |
| Indentation By | 1.02cm |
| Spacing Before | 0 |
| Spacing After | 0 |
| Line Spacing | Single |
| At | empty |
| **Tabs** ||
| Tab stop position: | 28.9pt |
| Alignment | Left |
| **Bullets and Numbering** ||
| Bulleted | Bottom right |
| Numbered | Bottom right |
| Outline Numbered | Bottom right |

Table 3. Settings for Heading 2.

| Heading 3 ||
|---|---|
| **Font** ||
| Font | Microsoft Sans Serif |
| Font style | Bold |
| Size | 12 |
| **Paragraph** ||
| General Alignment | Left |
| Outline level | Level 3 |
| Indentation Left | 0 |
| Indentation Right | 0 |
| Indentation Special | Hanging |
| Indentation By | 1.02cm |
| Spacing Before | 0 |
| Spacing After | 0 |
| Line Spacing | Single |
| At | empty |
| **Tabs** ||
| Tab stop position: | 38pt |
| Alignment | Left |
| **Bullets and Numbering** ||
| Bulleted | Bottom right |
| Numbered | Bottom right |
| Outline Numbered | Bottom right |

**Table 4. Settings for Heading 3.**

**Table 5 overleaf.**

| Heading 4 and 5 ||
|---|---|
| **Font** ||
| Font | Microsoft Sans Serif |
| Font style | Bold |
| Size | 12 |
| **Paragraph** ||
| General Alignment | Left |
| Outline level | Level 4 or 5 (whichever) |
| Indentation Left | 0 |
| Indentation Right | 0 |
| Indentation Special | Hanging |
| Indentation By | 1.52cm |
| Spacing Before | 0 |
| Spacing After | 0 |
| Line Spacing | Single |
| At | empty |
| **Tabs** ||
| Tab stop position: | 43.2pt (or 50.4pt for Heading 5) |
| Alignment | Left |
| **Bullets and Numbering** ||
| Bulleted | Bottom right |
| Numbered | Bottom right |
| Outline Numbered | Bottom right |

Table 5. Settings for Heading 4 and 5.

That completes all of the heading fonts. If you need to add a heading font you will need to click on the New Style button in the Style and Formatting right hand panel. Personally I avoid going beyond four levels of heading if I can, but in some documents you may need a fifth or a sixth level. Once you are beyond level three, keep all the font sizes the same size but change them to a bold typeface (size 12).

The other styles you will need to set up are Figure, Table and possibly Equation depending on your course subject; these however are all setup in a single font called 'Caption'. The settings are shown in Table 6.

| Caption + Centered (use this for Figure, Table and Equation) ||
|---|---|
| **Font** ||
| Font | Times New Roman |
| Font style | Bold |
| Size | 10 |
| **Paragraph** ||
| General Alignment | Centered |
| Outline level | Body text |
| Indentation Left | 0 |
| Indentation Right | 0 |
| Indentation Special | Hanging |
| Indentation By | empty |
| Spacing Before | 6pt |
| Spacing After | 0 |
| Line Spacing | Single |
| At | empty |
| **Tabs** ||
| Tab stop position: | empty |
| Alignment | Left |
| **Bullets and Numbering** ||
| Bulleted | None |
| Numbered | None |
| Outline Numbered | None |

Table 6. Settings for Caption + Centered styles.

Now that you have all your styles set up for producing your reports you need to save the file as (say) 'Report_template.doc' and it is suggested you keep a second copy somewhere else. This is the starting point for each of your reports. The first thing you do each time you begin a report is open this document and save it with a new name (use the Save As option) that is specific to the subject concerned. The reason you should keep a second copy is it is easy to forget to save it in the beginning before you start working and then mistakenly click on Save, you no longer have an empty document to use as a temple as it has now become a work in progress.

Inserting contents indexes or table of figures or other index is now a simple task of selecting Insert/References/Index and Tables from the menu and then finally OK to insert the table itself once you have made any adjustments to the table concerned in the GUI dialog. The only adjustment you are likely to need to make is the heading depth the contents table shows headings to. Generally you should use a full depth index for a contents table. So if you use headings to six levels deep you will need to set the Show levels digit to 6. I am not going to explain anything else in Word or other software package since you could keep going and going with numerous features for a number of software tools. If demand for the newsletter and forum website discussed at the beginning of this publication is promising it will become a regular feature in newsletters. (See http://www.1stacademy.net/supportnetwork.php )

### 4.2.4 Essay Writing

All coursework will open directly as a PDF file when the 1stAcademy site URL (http://www.1stacademy.net) is typed along with the path in the table. Alternately you can use the coursework index (http://www.1stacademy.net/courseworkindex.php). You will need Adobe Reader installed on your PC for this to work otherwise the PDF files will simply download and you will not be able to view them. Should you need to install Adobe Reader you should download it from the link on the index page and follow the instructions given. You should also bookmark this page on your browser.

| Coursework Examples for this section. ||
|---|---|
| Path: | \GradWith1stHons\Essays\Speculative Trading_Brief.pdf<br>\GradWith1stHons\Essays\Speculative Trading_Essay.pdf<br>\GradWith1stHons\Essays\When Science goes too far_Brief.pdf<br>\GradWith1stHons\Essays\When Science goes too far_Essay.pdf |
| Note: | Essay briefs (or questions) have been included allowing you to see both sides of the assessment. |

Many undergraduate courses have subjects where your university work will be assessed by essay – most essays are prepared in your own time over a period of days or weeks, however a subject may also include an examination essay that has to be written in the space of an hour or two. Therefore it must follow that learning how to prepare, organise and present quality essays will greatly improve your degree marks overall.

#### 4.2.4.1 Research

It is essential to spend time researching your essay topic. Find the things that interest you and which you would like to include in your essay. If you have a unique take on the topic you might want to run your ideas past the lecturer or another student. Another approach is to compare and contrast two or more ideas with others in your class. This often results in a new way of thinking that is outside the box.

### 4.2.4.2 Structure

Another key element is that of essay structure. It isn't enough to make sure that you have an introduction at the start, a conclusion at the end, and the other stuff in between. You need a solid introduction. It will probably contain details of how you have interpreted the question or essay topic. It is often a good idea to state a thesis (an argument) to be illustrated or explored in the body of the essay. Another technique is to save the 'findings' of your exploration to the end, in which case you have to introduce the question carefully at the start – so this is a style you may wish to adopt later on when you have gained experience.

A good essay will have a tight, powerful conclusion that is the logical consequence of everything that has been discussed throughout. Ideally you will have developed and contrasted a number of related threads that the conclusion will tie together. It may also contain an extra, surprising element which has been saved to throw in at the end with a flourish.

### 4.2.4.3 Body

Effective essays demonstrate the writer's breadth of knowledge – often with respect to contemporary issues, principles and practices – and ability to use language. The material you present needs to be organised so that it flows from one area, sub-section or argument to the next in a logical order. Each part should build upon, or at least reasonably follow on from, the previous parts, and the whole body should pull the reader, clearly and inescapably, towards the conclusion. A good approach is to look through your notes on the topic and identify a handful of themes to consider and structure your essay around the chosen themes. You should order the analysis of each theme so that the essay builds up towards the conclusion.

Begin with your notes from discussing the essay in class or from your research. Take a clean sheet of paper and begin by writing down phrases which summarise all of your thoughts, questions, ideas, problems and areas or considerations the topic has provoked. Then look for similarities and related concerns, and group them together in whatever order makes sense by numbering them as you progress (it is the numbered order that you are correlating, not the physical order that your items appear on paper). Thus the items you identify could be numbered: 1, 5, 4, 3, 6, 2, etc. from top to bottom. You now have a template that constitutes a logical progression (i.e. 1, 2, 3, 4, 5, 6, etc.) to follow when writing your essay. Once the essay is written, read through it and remove any superfluous words or phrases that have crept in, tweak the text so that it progresses in a crisp and consistent manner.

Before we move on, let's take a quick look at structures that are likely to result in low marks. Disorganisation of themes and threads is probably the quickest way to lose marks, so this makes a strong argument for following the approach discussed in the last paragraph. Avoid beginning with definitions of the subject or topic, followed by some material about the topic leading into a summary. Another approach to avoid is the formulaic approach: an introduction saying what will be discussed throughout, then citing a number of arguments in favour, followed by a number of arguments against, running into a summary of what went before.

### *4.2.4.4 Analysis*

Your ability to provide and contrast analysis in the body of your essay will dramatically increase your marks. You will often need to describe something before giving an analysis of it, but the more analysis you present the better. Only include as much description as is needed for the analysis to make sense. The analysis is what will get you marks, but your analysis needs to be consistent, coherent and concise, and supported by evidence. In general and where applicable, arguments and analyses of the ethos of nations, communities, business and industry, etc., is topical material that lecturers appreciate.

### *4.2.4.5 Don't digress*

Answer the question (or essay brief), and only the question. And keep checking that you are remaining on track throughout the essay – a good method is to select your text on screen and use the Word Count tool. If you now look at the word count and compare it to the required length of your essay relative to the material you have already addressed you can gauge whether you are on track or not. If there's something interesting that you want to include, but which is of dubious relevance to the main argument or theme, put it in a footnote, and remove it at the end if you're running over the word count.

You should always stay within an approximation of the count given; the tolerance can grow a little with the count. e.g. for a 2000 word essay the actual number of words could run between 1980 to 2020 words, but this should be checked with the lecturer.

### *4.2.4.6 Style as well as substance*

Whilst it would seem 'nice' if the ideas of a genius were appreciated even when written clumsily, you should not rely on this. The student who achieves a First not only has good ideas to write about, but can write about them well. And it seems particularly wasteful to be losing marks just because you didn't spend a little time developing your style (of course the best time to do this is in your first year when your marks don't count towards you graduation).

### 4.2.4.7 Can I write from my own perspective?

There are different preferences as to whether you should say "I" in an essay or not. Sometimes it can look good if you confidently say "Rather, I would argue that...". But saying "I feel this argument is wrong because..." can look a bit ponderous, and some lecturers dislike it. A solution to this is to be more assertive and say "However, this argument is weak, since...". It will still be clear that you are making your own argument, which is always desirable since it is your views the lecturer is interested in. Whatever you are saying, make sure you back it up with argument and evidence.

Finally, don't forget to make good use of 4.2.1 General Coursework assessment tips as all of these are relevant to essay writing.

## 4.2.5 Assignments

| | Coursework Examples for this section. |
|---|---|
| Path: | \GradWith1stHons\Year 2\Assignments\Application of Accounting Tech.pdf<br>\GradWith1stHons\Year 2\Assignments\Ass2QPSK.pdf<br>\GradWith1stHons\Year 2\Assignments\BatchMixerAss1.pdf<br>\GradWith1stHons\Year 2\Assignments\FIR Filter Design using MATLAB.pdf<br>\GradWith1stHons\Year 2\Assignments\Marketing and Motivation.pdf<br>\GradWith1stHons\Year 2\Assignments\Routing Problems.pdf<br>\GradWith1stHons\Year 3\Assignments\4by4Multiplier.pdf<br>\GradWith1stHons\Year 3\Assignments\Diagnosis System for Router.pdf<br>\GradWith1stHons\Year 3\Assignments\Digital Multimeter.pdf<br>\GradWith1stHons\Year 3\Assignments\Investigation of Routing Protocols.pdf<br>\GradWith1stHons\Year 3\Assignments\Microcontroller-Based Dongle.pdf<br>\GradWith1stHons\Year 3\Assignments\PC Patient Monitor.pdf<br>\GradWith1stHons\Year 3\Assignments\Real-time Operating System.pdf<br>\GradWith1stHons\Year 3\Assignments\Three Term controller.pdf |
| Note: | All assignments briefs are included (to allow you to see both sides of the assessments) and can be found via the same URL path as the assignments themselves. The briefs have the same file name as the assignment with the extension "_brief" on the end of the main file name. E.g. Ass2QPSK_brief.pdf. You may also view these from the coursework index. |

With assignments it's important to complete the work to the assignment brief. As a general guide, keep your paragraphs to between 5 to 12 lines; this assumes that your average sentence length is between one and a half lines. The length of sentences is important as long sentences make work harder to read. With this in mind, try to keep your longest sentences no longer than three lines and where possible, maintain an average length of one and a half lines. For example, note the average sentence length in this publication, you will see the same holds true.

The amount of writing the lecturer requires in an assignment will vary depending on the assignment itself. If you look at my assignments you will see that many of them have considerable write-ups while others have hardly any, therefore it is essential you are clear on the detail required for the write-up of each assignment.

Generally assignments will require a high degree of explanation in one form or another. However some of the low weighted assignments are almost like mini-assignments where the lecturer sets you a task to solve or a number of aspects to consider with a given subject, and you only have to work around a given criteria. Some briefs give a good starting point and may include work that is already done for you. Then there's the big assignments; the ones that are worth forty to fifty percent of your marks for a given subject. These are generally meaty assignments where you are expected to do something from scratch. In my case this usually involved designing a piece of electronic hardware (or circuit) or programming a computer program (or sometimes both), and then explaining how it works and how all the various aspects of said item were derived. There are a few of these meaty assignments in the examples provided with this publication.

To get a good feel for what is expected regarding length, detail and quality you should take a good look at all my assignments and relate this back to the net contribution weighting which is given in the descriptive tables in this book's website based appendices: Assignments for year 2, Assignments for year 3. You can then relate the level of detail in my assignments to the brief of your current assignment by reviewing my assignments with the same net contribution. Also, compare any of my assignments you single out as examples to the brief of your current assignment as a few of my assignments evolve around a single design or circuit, which in many cases will not make good examples for you. The contribution weighting will always be included in the assignment brief.

When you look through my assignments – and now would be a good time to begin – you will see some of them are thirty or more pages long. The reason for this with some assignments is they included program listings or hardware synthesis listings, or in the case of the networking assignment, lots of router COM reports that have been listed as text. So don't let this bother you – if an assignment needs to be that long it is likely to be so because you need to show the full extent of the work involved in the practical aspect of the assignment.

Many assignments will be based around class practical work sessions. My networking assignment 'An Investigation of Routing Protocols' (see website appendices Assignments for year 3) is a good example of this as the bulk of the assignment is the COM listings from the routers which we were asked to include in the brief to provide the evidence for the write up.

Also recap on what was said in 4.2 'How to present your coursework', as all of that material is highly applicable to assignments. To end this section a number of things you need to keep in mind or include when producing assignments are listed below.

1. In MS Word, select View/Toolbars/Drawing from the main menu. Position the toolbar somewhere comfortable for you when working on documents. At the bottom above the status panel is a good choice. You are likely to need these drawing tools a lot so you may as well have them to hand.

2. Include pictorial diagrams where they are helpful in gaining understanding of material presented. Generally, include as many as needed to address all the prominent aspects of the assignment and label them Figure 1, 2, etc. using the insert Caption (Insert/ Reference/ Caption) tool. The text that falls either before or after should of course relate to the figure concerned depending on whether it is more fitting to give a degree of explanation leading into showing the diagram, or more fitting to end one aspect and begin another with a diagram which you then explain. You should include a table of figures under the Contents index (Insert/References/Index and Table, Table of Figures tab).

3. There are a number of ways of creating pictorial diagrams, my personal favourite is Paint Shop Pro for the more complicated diagrams as it's a proper (but easy to use) graphics program that produces GIFs or JPEGs for importing into MS Word. Simple diagrams can be produced with the drawing toolbar in Word itself. It helps to make good use of the group, layering and behind/in front of text tools. Often when using the Word graphics tools you will want to turn off the Snap objects to grid option. It is suggested you customise the drawing toolbar (menu:

Tools/Customize) to include the grid tool and others (you will find all drawing tools in the Command tab within the Drawing category).

4. One of the most useful methods of creating diagrams – or more accurately, computer program still shots – is the Alt + Print Screen keys on your keyboard. If you're using a computer program like MatLab to design a computer model, you can grab the current window as a clipboard graphic using these keys at convenient stages throughout your design. You can then paste this image into your drawing software and annotate it ready for the write up in Word. This method makes really good diagrams. You may not need to annotate them, but you should use the drawing software to crop them to size. Remember a fair amount of text was spent discussing 'working smart'? Say you are modelling in MatLab prior to your assignment write up; using this window snapshot technique you can have all of your MatLab diagrams ready to start your write up at a later date saving valuable time. You will see how affective this technique is when looking at my work.

5. If needed, you can use floating label explanations to explain aspects of your diagrams. Do this by placing text in a textbox and positioning it in white space a little away from the diagram. You will need to format the textbox border to remove the line around the outside of the box (select the textbox by clicking at the edge and right click over the box and select Format Textbox, then adjust the Line Color option to None). Now you can draw an arrow from the floating label to the corresponding aspect on the diagram; the arrow can be found on the drawing toolbar. If you are annotating a GIF or JPEG (as apposed to an image drawn in Word) in this way you will need to select Tools/ Options from the menu and turn off 'Automatically create drawing canvas when inserting AutoShapes' on the General tab.

6. Also use floating textboxes with arrows pointing to text listing (the process is the same as explained in 5.) in any computer program listings that flow from page to page and anywhere else you think floating labels would help. (There are plenty of examples in my assignments. My Digital Systems Synthesis assignment '4by4Multiplier.pdf' makes good uses of this technique. If it proves impractical to use this technique because the width of a program listing is too long you can uses paragraphs in between segments of code. You may even want to combine both methods in places where needed.)

7. If you have a lot of text listings to display like my networking assignment

mentioned above, created a new label in Caption (Insert/Reference/ Caption, New label ) – I chose to call mine 'Chapter' in said assignment – and insert a label under each listing. You can then create a table of Chapters (or whatever) after the contents table or your table of figures. Textual listing like those in my routing assignment should be pasted into text boxes that are of a uniformed size throughout the assignment. It's also nice to put a border around each listing using the textbox border. Here's what you do: put your first listing in a textbox, select the textbox by clicking at the edge and right click over the box to select Format Textbox. Then adjust the Line option for the desired border. Make sure you are satisfied with the size etc of the border then use this textbox as a temple for every textbox to follow – just copy and paste and put the next text listing in the pasted textbox and position it.

8. Staying on the subject of computer program listings, make sure they are well commented throughout (see my code listings for good commenting practices). When you insert listings into Word and split them up into sections for explanation you can highlight the different components of the code and change them to the same colours they would appear in the programming editor. Again, these methods (and variations of them) are used in my C++ Object Oriented Programming assignment and group project report.

9. Try and simplify your explanations of diagrams or something technical as much as possible without leaving out information. Your explanations should be easy to follow whilst still imparting the elegance of your overall solution, design or whatever is being explained.

10. If you are taking a subject that involves a lot of maths equations use the Equation Editor in Word rather than attempt to type them on the page white space. It looks far more professional. It is suggested you select Tools/Customise from the Word menu and under Commands/ Insert, drag the Equation Editor icon onto a toolbar. You can also reach it via Insert/Object on the menu.

11. Always include a Bibliography at the end of your assignments listing all your various sources of information. You should include lecture notes/handouts, book titles and authors and internet URLs. You can split the Bibliography up into headings if applicable. You should begin with a bibliography heading when you start your assignment and add the source of any research you include throughout your text as you progress, otherwise you are liable to forget. Research included needs

to be written in your own words. Remember researched assignments generally score higher marks than those that are not.

12. Make good use of tables in your write up. Lecturers like tables that present information in an easy to understand format. Always begin your tables by making an assessment of how many columns and rows you will need and then create the table. You will probably need to improvise your tables, so select View/Toolbars/Table and Borders from the menu and doc the toolbar somewhere convenient.

13. Make good use of colours to highlight both parts of diagrams and important text points. Take a look at my Computer Networks assignment (see Coursework Examples at the beginning of this section for the file path), you will see that I highlighted important texts points from the COM text Chapters included in the assignment – for example, Chapter 11, 12, 13, 15, 16… and so on. This assignment was a write up of class practical sessions where a computer network was created and various tests were carried out. The highlighted text is used to identify the different results seen when carrying out the tests; this is the evidence on which the write up is based. With diagrams you can also use colours to create key maps making your diagrams easier to read; see pages 26 and 27 of my Major Project report for an example. There are plenty of examples of colour in diagrams throughout my work.

14. Use the header and footer on each page and page numbers, but not on the title page. If you look at my later assignments (certainly all in the third year) you will see the header displays the title of the assignment and the footer displays the title of the subject and the course – this will ensure a professional appearance. Access the header and footer via the View menu and the page number via the Insert menu. On the Page Numbers window you need to make sure the Show numbers on first page checkbox is unchecked – this will keep both the number and the header and footer from being displayed on the title page.

15. Always present your assignments with a clean and balanced title page. The format should be as follows: course title (48pt or smaller if the title is longer and takes up more than two lines at 48pt), the words 'Assignment' + assignment number for the given subject (in roman numerals looks good) (just 'Assignment' if there is only one, up to 26pt), the assignment title (18pt italic text), the course title (16pt), the university or institute name (16pt) and the words 'Lecturer:' followed by

their name (16pt), all centred. Your name should be at the bottom of the page (12pt right justified). See my title pages to get a feeling for a good balance regarding the physical length of titles versus font size. Adjust the font sizes given to achieve a balanced look where necessary.

16. Unless you are told differently an assignment should always end with a conclusion, and generally you will also have an 'introduction', unless it is more convenient to label the introduction as some other title. In some of my assignments the lecturers weren't concerned about finishing without a conclusion, this is most notably the Electronic Design subject as the focus was generally on the design of whatever it was; and we were told it wasn't needed.

17. The main body chapters should be arranged in a logical order, and unless there is good reason to deviate, it is best to organise the layout as the assignment evolves from start to finish.

18. When using abbreviations it is good practice to write the term in full first and then put the abbreviation afterwards between brackets. E.g. Routing Information Protocol (RIP) and Enhanced Interior Gateway Routing Protocol (EIGRP). After each term has been written once in full and the abbreviation has been placed between brackets you should then just use the abbreviation from then on. You may also include a 'Notations' section if you wish – although we were never asked to do this in the group project report, but it certainly wouldn't do any harm. See 4.2.9.7.3 Notations for details.

That concludes my formula for high mark yielding assignments – when looking through my assignments do keep in mind that I didn't perfect the layout until the third year. This is of course worthy of noting: it goes to prove it's the quality of the content that you produce that really counts. That is why the assignment examples are such a valuable part of this publication.

### 4.2.6 Preparing presentations (AKA Viva)

In a presentation, also commonly known as a Viva, OHP slides are typically produced in Microsoft PowerPoint and then either printed out on transparency film for use on an OHP or viewed as a PowerPoint presentation via a PC projector on a whiteboard.

The latter is my personal preference although both methods were used during my degree. What now follows is a guide for producing well balanced presentations (please keep in mind this is only a guide in that it is somewhat open to interpretation depending on your project subject).

Also, provide the lecturers present with handouts of your presentation as it lets the lecturers know you are treating it as a real presentation, which of course it is. You can easily produce handouts in PowerPoint by selecting Print and then setting the 'Print what:' dropdown to 'Handouts' and then configure it to the right for six slides per page vertically.

### 4.2.6.1 *How to plan an Interim Presentation*

| Coursework Examples for this section. ||
|---|---|
| Path: | \GradWith1stHons\Year 2\Group project\Assessment1\InterimVivaPres.pdf |
| | \GradWith1stHons\Year 3\Major Project\Assessment2\InterimVivaPres.pdf |

Interim Presentations are perhaps a little more difficult to prepare than final presentations, in that with the later you have the benefit of hindsight and a project report (even if not quite finished) to draw on, where as an interim presentation relies on good topic research, some careful planning and an element of prediction. One bonus: interim presentations are typically shorter than final presentations. To explain the procedure we will continue with numbered points.

1. Begin by preparing one to two introduction slides. Start by summarising the project objectives and then continue to address the details of the work to be completed to achieve the objectives.

2. Prepare a slide or slides that explain how you will begin the task of implementing your project – this might for example outline a design process if the project is an engineering task. The implementation of your project should at least be researched to a sufficient degree by this time.

3. The next set of slides should ideally breakdown the various development/implementation tasks of the project, and explain the theory behind the planned implementation. For example, in an engineering project these slides would explain how the project item works including theory.

4. If there are a number of possible implementation routes or choices also explain and justify these – this may precede the last bullet point; it depends on whatever works best with your project, you will have to decide this yourself.

5. By this time you should have two slides left, the first is a project plan or schedule which will almost certainly be a Gant chart. The lecturer will spend at least one lecture explaining your project plan and how to produce a Gant chart, so no explanation is necessary here.

6. Finally you will finish with a conclusion, which is probably going to be a brief summery of what you have done thus far and some forecasting (the element of prediction) of how the project should proceed. Do see my examples for a better understanding.

The above slides should be sandwiched between a cover slide and an end 'thank you' slide. Your lecturer will inform you of the ideal length of the presentation in terms of time, so don't exceed the upper limit. Remember, keeping to the time is favoured strongly, and the only way you will ever know how long your presentation takes is by practicing it a good number of times – see 4.2.6.3 Producing and memorising verbal content for detailed instruction. It is also possible that you may over budget in time if you have too many slides, so you may have to drop one slide and rethink the order/content of the slides to fix this.

The examples at the beginning of this section should be viewed with the accompanying text in 4.2.8.2 Assessment 1: Interim Group Presentation and 4.2.9.5 Accompanying files for group project respectively.

### *4.2.6.2 How to plan a Final Presentation*

| Coursework Examples for this section. ||
| --- | --- |
| Path: | \GradWith1stHons\Year 2\Group project\Assessment3\FinalVivaPres.pdf |
| | \GradWith1stHons\Year 3\Major Project\Assessment3\FinalViva.pdf |

Providing you have completed a good project, a final presentation should be relatively straightforward to prepare. The secret is to be organised with a strong project report as this is the source of all your slides. Let's look at some numbered points aimed specifically at final presentations:

1. Begin with Introduction slides that explain the project objectives and then continue to address the details of the work completed to achieve the objectives, thus setting up the presentation body material.

2. If required theory slide(s) should follow the introduction (theory is typically required in a third year Major Project and your project supervisor will make you aware of the required theory). Where possible keep technical theory in layman's terms, which makes the theory easier to understand, makes more effective use of time overall, leaves room for questions and respects that the lecturers sitting in on the presentation may not be experts in your subject area. Theory explanations should also link directly to your project. See 4.2.9.6 Assessment 3: Final Viva Voce for a good example of theory in a presentation.

3. For the bulk of the presentation that now follows, include the most relevant and impressive implementations in your project report.

4. Pay special attention to the explanation of problems you had to overcome, and details of solutions to said problems.

5. Towards the back end of the presentation it is time to think about wrapping up to a conclusion, so you now need to focus on the testing of the project or 'trials' as they are often referred to.

6. Always include a recap of the project plan or schedule before concluding (one slide only) and state how accurately the project went to plan (projects that go to plan are impressive as they demonstrate good planning). If your project went off course give a verbal account of why this happened and justify this as best you can. You can place an element of spin on any misfortunate occurrences to decrease the impact.

7. Finish with a thorough (and positive) conclusion detailing what was achieved (this should dwarf any implications of misfortunate occurrences you excused in 6) – again, draw on the conclusion from your report.

The above slides should be sandwiched between a cover slide and an end 'thank you' slide. Your lecturer will inform you of the ideal length of the presentation in terms of time, so don't exceed the upper limit. Remember, keeping to the time is favoured strongly, and the only way you will ever know how long your presentation takes is by practicing it a good number of times – see 4.2.6.3 Producing and memorising verbal content for detailed instruction.

It is also possible that you may over budget in time if you have too many slides, so you may have to drop one slide and rethink the order/content of the slides to fix this.

The examples at the beginning of this section should be viewed with the accompanying text in 4.2.8.4 Assessment 3: Final Group Project Presentation and 4.2.9.6 Assessment 3: Final Viva Voce respectively.

### 4.2.6.3 Producing and memorising verbal content

| Coursework Examples for this section. |
|---|
| Path: | \GradWith1stHons\Year 2\Group project\Assessment1\InterimVivaQcards.pdf<br>\GradWith1stHons\Year 2\Group project\Assessment3\FinalQcards.pdf |

The best technique for OHP or projector presentations is to effectively use the presentation slides to drive your presentation. It is vital that you don't 'ramble on' about your project; you need to give a specific delivery which is constructed around each of your slides. In order to formulate a structured verbal delivery you will first need to make some notes for each slide. Once you have the slides and a set of notes it is time to make a set of 'Qcards'.

In order to remember exactly what you want to say with each slide you will need to make Qcards to prompt you with regard to each point you need to talk about. You should also number the Qcards to correspond with the slides as it is likely that some slides will need more than one Qcard. Thus a given Qcard may be numbered: Slide 6, 1 of 2, or Slide 8, 2 of 3, etc.

Now you are ready to memorise your verbal content. You may want to use your study room floor for this next step. Place each slide together with its corresponding notes and Qcards – you can now commit one slide's verbal content to memory at a time. To do this read through the notes with each of the slides, noting the specific points on each slide's Qcard as you come to them in the notes. Do this repeatedly for each side. After you feel you may have done this sufficiently it is time to practice the presentation without your notes.

Keep practicing your verbal delivery for each slide using the corresponding Qcards to prompt you with the content to be vocalised. You will need to practice quite a lot to make it stick in your memory for a smooth delivery. Many students will maintain a methodical approach at this point (slide 1, slide 2, slide 3, etc.) – this is fine if it works for you. However I found it extremely effective to pick slides in a random pattern and then practice the delivery for that slide – you should be able to do this OK after practicing methodically for a while.

In time you will be able to deliver your verbal content without the Qcards, which you should also practice a number of times. Use the Qcards to prompt you should you forget an aspect of content. You can see some of my Qcards by opening the two files from the URL paths given on p53 – it looks like I produced my third year Qcards direct to card as I don't have a digital copy of them. It's also a good idea to practice delivering your presentation to another member of your group (if this is a group presentation) or to a fellow student to get the feel of delivering it to an audience.

### 4.2.7 Exams

| | Exam Examples for this section. |
|---|---|
| Path: | \GradWith1stHons\Exams (year 2&3)\Computer Networks\CN_Answers.pdf |
| | \GradWith1stHons\Exams (year 2&3)\Computer Networks\CN_Paper.pdf |
| | \GradWith1stHons\Exams (year 2&3)\ComunicationPrinciples\CP_Answers.pdf |
| | \GradWith1stHons\Exams (year 2&3)\ComunicationPrinciples\CP_Paper.pdf |
| | \GradWith1stHons\Exams (year 2&3)\Control and PLCs\C_PLCs_Answers.pdf |
| | \GradWith1stHons\Exams (year 2&3)\Control and PLCs\C_PLCs_Paper.pdf |
| | \GradWith1stHons\Exams (year 2&3)\Digital System Synthesis\DSS_addit.Q&A.pdf |
| | \GradWith1stHons\Exams (year 2&3)\Digital System Synthesis\DSS_Answers.pdf |
| | \GradWith1stHons\Exams (year 2&3)\Digital System Synthesis\DSS_Paper.pdf |
| | \GradWith1stHons\Exams (year 2&3)\Embedded Microcontroller Systems\EMS_Answers.pdf |
| | \GradWith1stHons\Exams (year 2&3)\Embedded Microcontroller Systems\EMS_Paper.pdf |

Exams are where many students come unstuck. It is not uncommon for students to do well with most of their coursework and then blow the chance of getting a First in the last couple of weeks of term in the third year. Some students say they are no good when it comes to exams, but I don't think that is the case. I find exams difficult myself yet I still got a First. The secret to overcoming this is to do two things: first, stay on top of your coursework from the very beginning so you have plenty of time to revise before exams and second, actually do the revision you planned.

Silly as it sounds, some students – like my fellow class mates mentioned earlier – do flitter their revision time away and then regret it. Others are not organised; because there is so much coursework to hand in in those last few weeks before exams they simply don't get enough time to revise. Clearly, some time for quality revision can make a world of difference!

So, what constitutes quality revision? Many students think it is enough to read through their notes a few times – frequently 'few' is the operative word – but I don't think it is. It's seems OK in revision but when the pressure is on the student invariably finds that reading alone doesn't cut it. They forget vital information, especially when time is against them in the last forty minutes. I think – or know in my case – the secret is to use the subject matter, to put into practice that which you have been taught. It is easy to put subject material into practice if you're taking an engineering or science subject – there are lots of equations and stuff you can practice with – but not so easy if you're taking (say) English History, when the course consists largely of content you must know.

Let's deal with subjects or topics that you have to know (or commit to memory) first. There are a couple of things you can do to make content stay in your mind. You can write the content into notes time and time again – this forces you to exercise your memory as opposed to just reading and hoping it somehow gets lodged in your mind. Read a few sentences or even a complete paragraph and then see how much you can regurgitate back to paper.

Another technique is to read and copy the content. Although it is superior to reading alone this is not stretching the memory that much. You are not making good use of the cognitive process as you are still in a low gear when really you should be giving it everything you've got. A better technique is to read and reconstruct the sentences or paragraphs so that they effectively say the same things but in a different way.

The second category, information that can be used constructively, is easier to lodge in memory. We all know that we learn best when we are engaged in activity – just watching others doing stuff is a poor substitute. So if for example, the subject is maths, you need to practice applying the equations and get to know them intimately by replacing the letters with numbers and transposing them on the fly to find values on ether side of the 'equal' symbol. If the subject is computer programming, bias towards solving problems or writing specific applications you can practice this on your computer and actually get code to work. I'm sure you have the idea and are able to apply your subject content without the need to add further examples.

A metaphor for all these techniques would be learning how to spell when you were a child. You didn't learn to spell by just reading did you? You read, and copied the words, and then you closed the books and wrote the words on paper. The teacher got you to write words from the previous day to see if you'd remembered them. You also practiced constructing words on paper you weren't sure if you were able to spell using your knowledge of how words sound and are constructed to make other words. If you tried to learn how to spell by just reading alone you'd probably still be learning now.

Almost all lecturers will let you know what subject material is likely to be in the exams. It is after all in their interest that as many students pass as possible – in fact most lecturers do one of three things: verbally tell you what will be in the exam and leave you to revise it, provide you with a list of topics to revise or give you a revision sheet with exam style questions to take away.

In Computer Networking in my final year our lecturer was kind enough to produce a nineteen question tutorial which was by far the best exam work up I have ever seen. I don't know what my final score was for that subject but I would think it was around seventy percent upwards, and this was one of my weaker subjects.

If you can possibly steer your lecturer in the direction of providing you with such a tutorial (if they are open to suggestion) then this is recommended. Should you get a list of topics or are verbally told which topics to revise, you could go through your notes and write a tutorial of your own which would also be excellent practice. Whether you choose to go down this route or not you should always create a set of revision notes. One of my techniques was to download previous papers (you should be able to do this via your university's intranet or Black Board system) and answer all the questions to create a set of notes that you can read through, and repeat the papers until they are lodged in your mind.

The predictable thing with exams is that they invariably evolve around a number of set topics; every year the lecturers select a number of topics from the pool of topics frequently used and then writes a new paper around them. Some of the questions in your paper will be close to those used in previous papers. You should always compare previous papers with the topics your lecturer asks you to revise – there is no point attempting questions that will not be in your paper.

The other great thing about this technique is not only does it allow you to work towards a set of notes; it identifies what you don't know or have forgotten. You can even highlight the questions you are having problems with and take the papers into your lecture and get some one to one tuition.

The only thing I would say is: be careful if you know the lecturer is new to teaching a given subject – if they have never taught the subject before then the pool of topics is liable to undergo some variation. And this also makes a strong case for double checking what information is liable to be present and whether or not your lecturer wrote the papers you are using for revision.

This brings me to the exam examples that come with this book; they are all previous year papers that I used to prepare myself for my exams. They are presented in two PDF files, one being the paper and the other the answers. Note: that on each I have answered all questions as opposed to following the instructions to only answer three. This is because I used the papers to construct revision notes, it is also the reason why some of my answers are typed rather than written by hand – this is more a question of what works best for you. Another thing I pay little attention to is practicing answering papers within the time limit – the important thing is to get the subject material to stay in your mind. By all means, try and stay within the time limit if it helps you, but personally I know I can always work faster when the knowledge is firmly in my mind.

As with all examples, they are included to show the length and depth to work to, but each paper also provides a good example of building a set of revision notes to work with. Finally, because this is a lot of information in a condensed space here is a set of bullet points to recap:

- Stay on top of coursework throughout the year so you have plenty of time to revise.
- Resist the temptation to fritter time away.
- Practise putting the subject matter to use to solve problems or answer mock questions.
- Create your own mock questions or better still, try and get your lecturer to provide mock questions as a tutorial.
- Download exams from previous years from your university intranet or Black Board and practice answering all questions.
- Check that the question topics of previous papers are to be used in your paper and ask if your lecturer wrote all the papers you downloaded.
- Work towards preparing a set of exam revision notes (note: in some cases these may be computer generated if that works best for

you), write them out time and time again and practice regurgitating them from memory to paper.
- Practice reading and reconstruct your classroom notes and handouts.
- Practice any computer subjects like programming or using applications (if this is likely exam material) on your computer – more importantly, get it working on the computer.
- Look through all my exam examples to get the feel of the correct length and detail depth to work to.

## 4.2.8 Group Project (second year)

### *4.2.8.1 Overview*

The Group Project is in many ways a prequel for the Major Project in Year Three, so it serves a part purpose to prepare you for the Third Year Project. It helps you get to grips with project management and planning. Another aspect is to improve your team working skills. I can only give you an account on the group project from my personal experience, but this does not really matter as your lecturer will brief you fully on what he or she requires. The fact that you can read my interpretation is a bonus since it comes from the student angle as opposed to that of the lecturer.

Before taking a look at a number of important group project aspects and issues it is important some consideration be given to project planning. Your lecturer will spend a fair amount of time with you discussing the planning of your project and how to depict it in a Gant Chart. From the group project plan you will also derive a personal project plan that too will be depicted in a Gant Chart. It is not necessary for us to discuss this further, but the one important point I wish to make is this: once you have a group project plan and a personal project plan derived, based on the information given by your lecturer, be sure to stick to them and don't allow yourself to fall behind relative to your personal plan. Also try to impress upon the members of your group to stick to the project plan. There is of course no problem with being ahead of the plan, if this can be managed it is a big plus.

We'll begin by examining the group project brief, and keep in mind, there are likely to be a number of parallels between the brief I received and the brief you will receive when you begin. The first thing to note is that the overall project is weighted at 100% contribution – nothing unexpected in that, but keep in mind that over the course of the project there will be a number of pitfalls that can lose marks for you. You should understand that because you are being marked by the project assessment vehicle route, it is really quite different from essay, assignment and exam vehicles that you are used to in other subjects.

Let's examine the differences before we continue to ensure you are better equipped to avoid a few potential pitfalls. A successful project that comes together and yields high marks for group members is dependent on a stream of events throughout the course of the project (typically in the professional world these are referred to as project milestones). The normal essay, assignment or exam vehicles are more forgiving in that when you are given (say) an assignment you have the opportunity to draw from your class notes and other areas of research to produce a good assignment. The same is true of exams with regard to the revision period. With a project, if something goes wrong at a specific point it tends impact throughout the rest of the project.

Let's consider an analogy to help your understanding. Think of the group project as a game of football – for a football team to win a match a number of things have to come together at the right time. If the team begins to make a number of bad moves (or errors) from the outset they are automatically put in a weak position – before the team know it a number of goals are scored against them and they fall behind. If your project runs into trouble because it is falling behind schedule (in much the same way as in the analogy) it will be more difficult to extract good marks in the various assessments. Actually, an engineering project is a good example because if the project is in a healthy position the group has a better opportunity to get the project working, and if it works it will be more impressive for the lecturers. The group will also be able to present their final reports and presentation with maximum coverage because they completed the project effectively.

Groups that fail to conclude their project are therefore at a disadvantage with the two final assessments (which incidentally carry the highest marks). Also, revisiting the analogy, all players on the team have to pull their weight and play in harmony as a team. If a minority of team members let their side down by playing sloppy football, again, the team is automatically in a weak position and goals are scored against them – the same applies to the group project, but we'll look at the team element in more detail to see how hazards can be avoided.

This is why it is very important to keep up to date with your project segments and impress upon fellow team members to do the same. Let's take a look at my project brief. We'll begin with a segment of the 'Assessment/Coursework Specification' – information not important to this discussion has been omitted.

| Outcomes being Assessed ||
|---|---|
| Assessment numbers | Description |
| 1, 2 & 3 | Plan a project, identify necessary resources and organise its implementation within a given period. Demonstrate personal contribution to project. Demonstrate an end product and justify its details. |

| Common Skills (Key Skills) assessed ||
|---|---|
| 1 | Managing and Developing Self |
| 2 | Working with and Relating to Others |
| 3 | Communicating |
| 4 | Managing Tasks |
| 5 | Applying Numeracy |
| 6 | Applying Technology |
| 7 | Applying Design and Creativity |

**Table 7. Areas of assessment, number of assessment vehicles and project description.**

Here we see the group project brief is setting three vehicles (or methods) of assessment as well as providing a short description of what is expected of each project group. Finally the table names the common or 'key stills' the three assessments will be assessing. Let's continue by examining some more information given to us along with the brief sheet.

| Design Studies / Group Project |
|---|
| The purpose of the Group Project is to develop group working qualities and enhance the Engineering Application skills developed during Year 1 of the course. This is achieved by undertaking a design task requiring the cost effective solution of a relevant industrial/commercial or educational problem. |
| The vehicle used for this purpose is the Group Project whereby the student is required to work with and co-operate with other students towards achieving a set objective. |
| Students will work in groups to design and implement a workable solution to a stated problem. A number of lectures will precede the project in order to prepare the students for the design task. Following the lectures specification for the project will be given and the group structure will be defined. |
| The project will be assessed in stages, the following page outlines the assessment strategy. |

> ### Assessment Strategy
>
> Assessment will be in three parts:
>
> Assessment 1 will be completed before the Christmas break. (Nov/Dec)
> Assessment 2 will be completed in early May.
> Assessment 3 will be completed by the end of May.
> NB: These are tentative dates and exact dates will be provided latter in the year..
>
> ASSESSMENT 1: INTERIM VIVA / PROGRESS REPORT
>
> This will take the form of a verbal presentation where each student will contribute to a progress report introducing the project, describing the overall project plan and assessing the progress of the project. The assessment will be aimed at the verbal (and the visual aids) communication skills of the student. Also, a group mark will be given for the group cohesiveness and efficiency. NB: You will be required to produce your own personal project plan which is to be derived from the overall plan. THIS IS TO BE SUBMITTED AT THE INTERIM VIVA.
>
> A total of 20% of total marks will be given for this assessment.
> 15% will be given for individual contribution and the remaining 5% will be given for the level of group cohesiveness and efficiency. NB: All members of the group will get the same mark for this part of the assessment.
>
> ASSESSMENT 2: PROJECT REPORT
>
> 45% of the marks will be for an individual project report, submitted in advance of the final viva.
>
> ASSESSMENT 3: FINAL VIVA
>
> 30% will be allocated for individual personal contribution (assessed at Viva).
>
> 5% will be allocated, as a common mark, for the completed project.

**Table 8. Additional double sided information sheet handed out with the project brief.**

OK, so we have some useful information here to discuss with an aim of making some constructive points of things to be aware of, or careful of, and things we can do to avoid losing marks should the project suffer.

What deductions or observations can we draw from this information?
1. The purpose of the Group Project is to develop group working qualities and enhance skills developed during the first year of your course (keep this point in mind when considering points 8 and 11).

2. The design task is to be undertaken with a view to achieving a cost effective solution (question: why?).

3. A specification for the project will be given and the group structure defined after a set of lectures. (The later is of more interest. Group structure is referring to who you will be working with and your role within the group, or to put it another way, the project segments you are responsible for. Typically there will be two to three students in each group.)

4. The project is assessed in three stages (a rough timetable is provided), an Interim Viva presentation, a Project Report and a Final Viva presentation. (We can now examine each of these to open out our deductions and observations.)

5. Assessment 1 (inc. points 6, 7 & 8): Each student will contribute in the verbal presentation detailing the project plan (this refers to the implementation and is represented via a Gant chart) and the progress thus far using visual aids (MS Power Point slides or presentation).

6. The assessment is aimed at (or more accurately put, you will be assessed on) verbal communication skills and quality of visual aids.

7. Each student is required to discuss their own personal project plan, which has been derived from the overall project plan.

8. A maximum of 20% can be awarded for this assessment, 15% of which is rewarded on an individual basis and 5% on a group basis (specifically for the way the group works as a team). Interestingly, the remaining 5% reflects on all members equally, which is good for you if your group is a cohesive and efficient unit or bad if the group is ineffective and detached.

9. Assessment 2: A maximum of 45% is awarded for you individual project report.

10. Assessment 3 (inc. point 11): A maximum of 30% will be awarded for individual personal contribution in the Final Viva presentation.

11. A maximum of 5% is awarded to each individual for a complete project – note this is a common mark, so again it will reflect on all members the same.

From the above points let's make a number of observations, especially regarding potential hazards, and derive an operating strategy to fend off the loss of marks based on the inherent hazards of the group project vehicle. The observations and strategy tactics to protect against hazards are tied to the numbered points above by a number placed in square brackets.

We are informed of the purpose of the group project, but more importantly it is clear that emphasis is placed on the student's ability to work collectively as a team [1] – meaning some of the marks you accrue individually are common to all members and depend on how good a team you make [8 & 11].

This is something to be cautious of because other members can now lose you marks. If, for example, a member of your team is disruptive it will be evident that the team does not function well together and you will lose a few marks specifically for that reason. But, again revisiting the football analogy, it is worse than that. If the team does not work effectively together it will impact throughout the project meaning you may not be able to maximise on your individual mark quotient. The project is likely to be incomplete making it difficult for you to demonstrate that you worked on your segment(s) to the best of your ability.

The reason it becomes difficult to maximise on individual mark quotients [9 & 10] with an incomplete project is in many projects each group member's segment(s) is liable to be dependent on the other member's segment(s) – this is especially relevant to engineering or computer science projects. It can be particularly difficult if the only way to really prove your segment(s) function correctly is for the project to function as a whole. Clearly, it would be beneficial to have a strategy that allows you to maximise your marks if such an outcome should arise.

There was quite a lot of emphasis on a cost effective solution in our group project [2], the reason being: engineering is a subject of industry, which is nearly always based around businesses that exist to make money. Thus, it is logical to consider many projects in industry don't really come about as a means to solve a problem; they come about as a means of making money by creating a product that solves a problem. This is an important distinction to keep in mind as most engineers have to work within these confines. No business wants a solution that isn't cost effective, because profit is not being maximised. Hence, this was an aspect we had to adhere to if we were to maximise our marks, and you may well have to operate under the same consideration.

The project specification will define the achievements you and the group must satisfy in order to score maximum marks [3], so this is vital. You will receive a specification for your group project, you must impress upon the group to follow it, or at the very least, make sure your work meets that specification. With regards to group structure, the lecturer is likely to divide you into groups as opposed to letting you choose who you want to work with. They will mostly likely do this to try and achieve balanced groups, i.e. avoid groups that consist of only strong or weak students.

Each project suggestion provided by the lecturer will then be considered by the groups, and I suggest you play an active role in choosing a project – a choice that sounds interesting and achievable to you. Once each group has a project, the project will then be divided into segments by the group members, with assistance from the lecturer who will have a good idea of what separate segments the project should be split into. Again, I suggest you make it known which segment of the project you want to tackle, if you have a preference, before another member discounts it by claiming it theirs.

A timetable is provided which of course you must adhere to yield as many marks as possible [4]. Your timetable is likely to be comparable to that shown here. We are told what elements of the project plan and progress thus far each student must present in the verbal assessment [5]. Specifically we need to consider how you should prepare for your verbal presentation as it is very important that you are clear on what you need to say and what visual aids you need [6 &7].

To ensure your work can yield maximum marks even if others' performance has a detrimental effect on the overall effort we first need to identify the areas such a strategy can be effective in. Other than trying to appeal to the better nature of other team members there is nothing we can really do to boost the common mark elements [8 & 11] should your group performance be impaired by others. Remember this is only 10% so it is more efficient to concentrate on maximising individual marks [8, 9 &10].

So the question becomes: how can you protect your individual mark quotient if the team effort is suffering from poor performance from another team member? The answer is simple enough: although the group is considered a team and each member has their own project segment to produce, you also need to prototype or emulate elements of other member's segments that your segment is dependent on. Basically, you produce a 'workaround' of any element in another member's segment you need to prove the completion of your own segment. This will become more evident when we examine my group project.

### 4.2.8.2 Assessment 1: Interim Group Presentation

| | Coursework Examples for this section. |
|---|---|
| Path: | \GradWith1stHons\Year 2\Group project\Assessment1\InterimVivaPres.pdf |
| | \GradWith1stHons\Year 2\Group project\Assessment1\InterimVivaQcards.pdf |

Your group will present Assessment 1 together as a presentations; each member will speak in turn depending on a planed schedule. The most important thing with the presentation is advance planning; this is planning that you will do largely by yourself, since you speak separately, but naturally there will be an element of group planning to decide the appropriate order for you to speak in. Earlier in 4.2.6 Preparing presentations we discussed how to prepare an Interim slide presentation; this is the key to your presentation, as explained, these slides effectively drive your presentation.

If your interim presentation follows the same format as mine there will be around ten slides; your lecturer will inform you of the duration and the approximate number of slides needed. It is important to have good slides that give you a reasonable amount to talk about per slide. To continue this discussion we will now use my group project as an example, which is good because this project was very successful. The lecturers were thrilled when we demonstrated our PC controlled robot arm working at the end of the project.

In my group project there were two of us and the project itself was to design a PC interface to operate and control the motors of a robotic arm. The interface clearly divided into four distinct segments:

1. A PC program to send control codes via the COM port to a control circuit (which divided into the remaining segments).

2. A voltage conversion sub-circuit to limit the levels transmitted from the PC COM port output as the voltage exceeds that of the electronics it is to be connected to.

3. A decoder sub-circuit to decode which of the five motors to activate based on the data transmitted by #1.

4. And a motor drive segment to switch battery power to the appropriate motor within the robot arm.

At this stage you need to look at my interim group presentation (see the file path given at the beginning of this section) to continue this discussion. Scroll down to slide three, you will see a slide titled Block Diagram of Overall Control System which divides the project into five segments; ignore the segment named Robot Arm Motors since this only constitutes the robot arm itself which we had to plug our interface into. You can now see the four segments I referred to earlier titled: PC/VB Control Program [1], Voltage Conversion [2], PIC Microcontroller [3] and Motor Drive Circuitry [4]. Let's take a look at how we arrived at the respective slides in this presentation to demonstrate how a typical project might be broken down into slides for the interim presentation.

| | |
|---|---|
| Slide1 | is the group project title slide during which we introduced ourselves. |
| Slide2 | is an Introduction. Again, you will need one of these. This simply breaks the project down into four segments, introduces each segment and the specific design task related to each segment. |
| Slide3 | shows the overall project divided into the respective segments. |
| Slide4 | introduces the robot arm and its functionality, as well as a task that we must undertake to begin our design. That is the tracing of the motor wiring. Also note: we have chosen to work backwards from the robot arm towards the PC. This is an equally logical course of action to working forwards for our project since it allowed us to examine what electronics (and transmission codes) would be needed to work the robot arm. |
| Slide5 | shows a representation of the motor drive segment circuit and effectively explains what it does and the fact that the circuit is a repetition of five duplicated circuits. It also states when the development of the segment will commence. |
| Slide6 | shows the decoder segment which is a PIC Microcontroller and explains what it does. Again, the status of that segment is given, saying that the PIC control code will not be programmed until completion of the circuit schematic. |

| Slide7 | shows the Voltage Conversion segment and explains what it does and what component we intend to use for the job. |
|---|---|
| Slide8 | this shows a mock up of the Graphic User Interface (GUI) that will be used to control the robot arm from the PC. The slide also states the next stage in the development of the GUI and when that will commence. |
| Slide9 | shows the Group Project Schedule or Project Plan as it is often referred to. This takes the form of a Gant chart. Your lecturer will give you a lot of instruction on how to develop this as it is a vital part of the project – they will give you specific instruction on the various task timing etc, so we won't discuss this any further. |
| Slide10 | is a conclusion, you will also need one of these. Again, use mine as an example to base yours on as it is a thorough conclusion. |
| Slide11 | is simply an end slide – again you will need one and you may as well copy it. |

Once you have produced your slides each member then has to work out what they have to talk about with each slide. There are likely to be a number of slides where you will say nothing while your other group members speak about their respective segment(s), and there will probably be a number of slides where it is appropriate that each member talks in turn. Remember with my group project there were two of us: on some slides we both spoke and others only one of us spoke. For example: see my Qcards for this assessment, you can see I spoke on slides 1, 3, 4, 5, 8 and 9 and the other team member spoke alone on the omitted slides – she also would have spoken on some of the slides I spoke on.

### *4.2.8.3 Assessment 2: Group Project Report*

| Coursework Example for this section. ||
|---|---|
| Path: | \GradWith1stHons\Year 2\Group project\Assessment2\ProjectReport.pdf. |

To help you develop your own project report we will take a close look at my report and the team's project to further demonstrate how the two items tie together. This will also demonstrate how and why the project was so successful. We will proceed in the order of flow of my report. You can find my project report by following the URL path given above. This section uses square bracketed index numbers throughout to tie the analyses to the Project Report example.

I begin the report by providing a short but comprehensive description of the project itself [2] – this sets the scene. An introduction then follows; this in the most part evolves around two elements, a block diagram of the project (the 'segments') and the group project plan [3.2]. The introduction begins by describing how the project was divided into segments and displays who was responsible for each segment in the diagram. Let's take a closer look at each of the blocks [3.1].

1. PC running a VB Control Program – a program has to be devised to send signals to the computer's COM port via a GUI, which also has to be design as part of the overall project (my partner).

2. Voltage conversion of RS232 levels to TTL levels. This is a simple circuit that anyone can easily find by Googling the title of the block. The easiest method is to use a single integrated circuit designed for the job (myself).

3. PIC microcontroller decoder. This is more involved, like the PC VB program. The circuit itself is simple enough and there is no shortage of web pages that demonstrate how to connect a PIC microcontroller. The reason the circuit is simple is everything complicated is preformed by a single firmware program (or software) running inside the microcontroller (myself).

4. Motor drive circuit – this again is fairly straight forward in that it is a repartition of a simple transistor and relay circuit. There is a slightly complex element in that the circuit has to allow for the reverse connection of every robot arm motor allowing each motor to spin in both directions. This is achieved by a sixth transistor relay circuit which reverses the polarity of the battery voltage that is being fed to each motor by the respective On/Off control relay (my partner).

From the segment descriptions you can see the workload is comparatively split: we both have a software program of some description to write (mine will run on the PIC microcontroller) and I have two simple circuits to build. My partner also has a circuit to build which has straightforward elements, but is repetitive in nature and requires some clever relay wiring to reverse the battery voltage to the robot arm motors. All quite fairly distributed.

My introduction continues with a summary of a remaining element of the project that was being left open at the time for a matter of convenience: The robot arm had what looked to be rather a strange wiring scheme between the battery and the motors, and there was some debate as to how our electronics would be integrated between the two and whether or not the electronics could be powered by said batteries. My task within the overall project was then explained (pay close attention to this) and I subtly state that I need to explore an element of one of my partner's segments. This is of course vital to getting my own segments working and avoids possible delays for me (due to the inherent hazard of the 'team element' of the project). It can later be see that I 'prototyped' my own PC COM port test program [7.1].

Incidentally, my partner needs to emulate my PIC microcontroller decoder circuit if the Motor Drive Circuit segment is to be tested without my segments; this was done by using a bank of switches and a power source to trigger the inputs to the sub-circuit. It worked flawlessly. Also I need to provide a method for emulating my partner's drive motor section, this is achieve by using LEDs [7.2.2] that light up in place of motors spinning when the Drive Circuits are engaged. Clearly both of us are addressing the necessity of being able to work alone.

The introduction concludes with some recapping of the interim presentation and a discussion around the group project plan [3.2]. Incidentally, if you take a closer look at the group project plan you will see that we allowed five weeks starting from the 8th of April to complete our project reports. In practice I began my report early during the development of my decoder circuit and firmware segment which aided my staying on top of my workload throughout the busiest period of the last semester. I suggest you do the same, as you have the various elements of your segments finalised, write them up. For example: begin a report while you are researching elements of the project and add the research elements you decide to use.

The next chapter [4], Initial Ideas and Research, begins by researching elements of my VB test program (for the PC) which is justified by taking a look at a Microsoft example and stating it enables testing of decoding theories [4.1]. Also, before developing the decoder, researching the PC COM signals on the internet that the decoder is to decode and convert into motor drive signals would later prove useful [4.2].

The rest of this research chapter concentrates on a number of aspects relevant to my two segments which you can read for yourself to give you an idea and feel for the level of detail you should include in your research chapter. When you read this chapter pay careful attention to the various justifications used to choose the various elements of the overall solution. Lecturers like to see these elements and as discussed every justification, especially with regard to cost were a big concern with our group project.

Next a specification for the decoder is provided (this includes the RS232 voltage conditioning sub-circuit); the two segments are now being conveniently packaged into an overall segment [5.1-5.3]. Presumably your group project will have a specification too, or an equivalent to it depending on the subject you study. An overall circuit diagram of the robot arm/PC interface showing my partner's circuit segment as a single block then follows [6]. Your project is likely to have an equivalent to this circuit diagram in one form or another. This chapter concludes with a component list – something your project will also have an equivalent of if it is physical in nature.

The report then continues with my decoder design process beginning with a brief description of my VB test GUI software [7.1] and a full listing of the software code. I justify leaving out details of how the software was developed by stating it is purely a tool to aid the development of the decoder. Another reason for leaving out the development process is it would be wrong to present work that could be compared and contrasted against the work presented in my partner's report. In practice, my partner's PC program turned out to be vastly different to my test program and looked like an animated XBOX control pad. It would have been equally logical for her to begin the design process by stating how she was going to emulate my decoder in order to provide the input signals necessary to test her motor drive circuit. Many project managers would agree it makes good sense to exercise an element of overlapping in team projects where possible.

Next follows the beginnings of the decoder build as the RS232 to TLL conversion segment was built on its own [7.2.1]. This is to allow a practical test of the circuit so that the TTL signal that the microcontroller needs to decode can be seen on an oscilloscope. This section is essentially a mini test write up. The next two sections of the chapter [7.2.2-7.2.3] includes the theory and calculations regarding the use of various circuit configurations and components. The chapter closes with the circuit board layout for the prototype decoder [7.2.4].

The next chapter of my report [8] details the devising of the RS232 Control Code Scheme which in layman's terms is identifying a simple computer instruction transmission scheme (or technique) that my decoder was cable of decoding and substituting equivalent motor control drive signals as I/O port outputs. This in practice was a little tricky due to unforeseen timing fluctuations and hence, my first attempt at devising a control code scheme failed as is reflected in the text. My second attempt is however successful [8.2], thus I can continue the report with a full explanation of how the overall embedded software control program will interpret the PC communications. The next chapter [9] begins by discussing the PIC microcontroller program flow and a number of flowcharts are included to simplify the program logic and operations [9.1.1-9.1.4]. The flowcharts are followed with a full examination of the program code [9.2.1-9.2.9], which is displayed in segments and then explained in paragraph text. This chapter finishes with a full listing of the PIC decoder control program, which takes the report up to page 38. Following this the project concludes with a conclusion [10] and a bibliography [11].

Since the analyses of my report is now complete let's take a look at some useful tips for writing a concise and well detailed project report. These tips also included references to one or two assignments to demonstrate useful techniques.

1. If you have not already done so, in MS Word, select View/Toolbars/Drawing from the main menu. Position the toolbar somewhere comfortable for you when working on documents. At the bottom above the status panel is a good choice. You are likely to need these drawing tools a lot so you may as well have them to hand.

2. Include pictorial diagrams where they are helpful in gaining understanding of material presented. Generally, include as many as needed to address all the prominent aspects of the project document and label them Figure 1, 2, etc. using the insert Caption (Insert/Reference/Caption) tool. The text that falls either before or after should of course relate to the figure concerned depending on whether it is more fitting to give a degree of explanation leading into showing the diagram, or more fitting to end one aspect and begin another with a diagram which you then explain. You should include a table of figures under the Contents index (Insert/References/Index and Table, Table of Figures tab).

3. There are a number of ways of creating pictorial diagrams, my personal favourite is Paint Shop Pro for the more complicated diagrams as it's a proper (but easy to use) graphics program that produces GIFs or JPEGs for importing into MS Word. Simple diagrams can be produced with the drawing toolbar in Word itself. It helps to make good use of

the group, layering and behind/in front of text tools. Often when using the Word graphics tools you will want to turn off the Snap objects to grid option. It is suggest you customise the drawing toolbar (menu: Tools/Customize) to include the grid tool and others (you will find all drawing tools in the Command tab within the Drawing category).

4. One of the most useful methods of creating diagrams – or more accurately, computer program still shots – is the Alt + Print Screen keys on your keyboard. If you're using a computer program like MatLab to design a computer model, you can grab the current window as a clipboard graphic using these keys at convenient stages throughout your design. You can then paste this image into your drawing software and annotate it ready for the write up in Word. This method makes really good diagrams. You may not need to annotate them, but you should use the drawing software to crop them to size. Remember a fair amount of text was spent discussing 'working smart'? Say you are modelling in MatLab prior to your project write up; using this window snapshot technique you can have all of your MatLab diagrams ready to start your write up at a later date saving valuable time. You will see how effective this technique is when looking at my work.

5. If needed you can use floating label explanations to explain aspects of your diagrams. Do this by placing text in a textbox and positioning it in white space a little away from the diagram. You need to format the textbox boarder to get rid of the line around the outside of the box (select the textbox by clicking at the edge and right click over the box and select Format Textbox, then adjust the Line Color option to None). Now you can draw an arrow from the floating label to the corresponding aspect on the diagram; the arrow can be found on the drawing toolbar. If you are annotating a GIF or JPEG (as apposed to an image drawn in Word) in this way you will need to select Tools/ Options from the menu and turn off 'Automatically create drawing canvas when inserting AutoShapes' on the General tab.

6. Also use floating textboxes with arrows pointing to text listing (the process is the same as explained in 5.) in any computer program listings that flow from page to page and anywhere else you think floating labels would help. My Digital Systems Synthesis assignment '4by4Multiplier.pdf' makes good uses of this technique, but in my group project report it proved impractical to use them as the width of the

program listing was too long. Instead paragraphs in between segments of code were used. You may even want to combine both methods in places where needed.

7. Staying on the subject of computer program listings, make sure they are well commented throughout (see my code listings for good commenting practices). When you insert listings into Word and split them up into sections for explanation you can highlight the different components of the code and change them to the same colours they would appear in the programming editor. Again, these methods (and variations of them) are used in my C++ Object Oriented Programming assignment and group project report.

8. Try and simplify your explanations of diagrams or something technical as much as possible without leaving out information. Your explanations should be easy to follow whilst still imparting the elegance of your overall solution, design or wherever is being explained.

9. If you are taking a subject that involves a lot of maths equations use the Equation Editor in Word rather than attempt to type them on the page white space. It looks far more professional. It is suggested you select Tools/Customise from the Word menu and under Commands/Insert, drag the Equation Editor icon onto a toolbar. You can also reach it via Insert/Object on the menu.

10. Always include a Bibliography at the end of your report listing all your various sources of information. You should include lecture notes/handouts, book titles and authors and internet URLs. You can split the Bibliography up into headings if applicable. You should begin with a bibliography heading when you start your report and add the source of any research you include throughout your text as you progress, otherwise you are liable to forget. Research included needs to be written in your own words. Remember researched reports generally score higher marks than those that are not. If you are asked to include a Reference section, which is really a stricter bibliography, be sure to ask if you are expected to include both or whether the reference section will suffice. Be sure you clarify the exact differences between the two with your lecturer.

11. Make good use of tables in your write up. Lecturers like tables that

present information in an easy to understand format. Always begin your tables by making an assessment of how many columns and rows you will need and then create the table. You will probably need to improvise your tables, so select View/Toolbars/Table and Borders from the menu and doc the toolbar somewhere convenient.

12. Make good use of colours in diagrams and to highlight important computer print out text if applicable. In my group project report (see website appendices: Group Project for the file path) colour is use in a program listing so that the code appears as it would in the editor allowing the variables and commands to stand out easily. With diagrams you can also use colours to create key maps making your diagrams easier to read; see pages 26 and 27 of my Major Project report for an example (see website appendices: Major Project for the file path). There are plenty of examples of colour in diagrams throughout my work.

13. Use the header and footer on each page and page numbers, but not on the title page. The header should display the title of your group's project and the title of your project segment(s) and the footer should display your subject, i.e. 'Group Project' and the course title – this will ensure a professional appearance. Access the header and footer via the View menu and the page number via the Insert menu. On the Page Numbers window you need to make sure the Show numbers on first page checkbox is unchecked – this will keep both the number and the header and footer from being displayed on the title page.

14. Always present your project report(s) with a nice clean and balanced title page. The format should be as follows: project title (48pt or smaller if the title is longer and takes up more than two lines at 48pt), your course title (20pt), the subject, i.e. 'Group Project' (20pt), the university or institute name (20pt) and the words 'Lecturer:' followed by their name (16pt), all centred. Your name should be at the bottom of the page (12pt right justified). See my title pages to get a feeling for a good balance regarding the physical length of titles versus font size. Adjust the font sizes given to achieve a balanced look where necessary.

15. Always start your report with an introduction and finish with a conclusion. The introduction will introduce the project and set the document up for the explanations and descriptions to follow. The conclusion assess

the techniques used to solve or construct your project segments and the level of success you achieved – it should also touch on important or key elements of the project. For example, my conclusion finishes by citing that all the constrains of quality versus affordability with a view to mass manufacturing where met. Remember this was a key element in my project.

16. The main body chapters should be arranged in a logical order, and or less there is good reason to deviate, it is best to organise the layout as the project evolved from start to finish.

17. When using abbreviations it is good practice to write the term in full first and then put the abbreviation afterwards between brackets. E.g. Routing Information Protocol (RIP) and Enhanced Interior Gateway Routing Protocol (EIGRP). After each term has been written once in full and the abbreviation has been placed between brackets you should then just use the abbreviation from then on. You may also include a 'Notations' section if you wish – although we were never asked to do this in the group project report, but it certainly wouldn't do any harm. See 4.2.9.7.3 Notations for details.

### *4.2.8.4 Assessment 3: Final Group Project Presentation*

| Coursework Examples for this section. | |
|---|---|
| Path: | \GradWith1stHons\Year 2\Group project\Assessment3\FinalVivaPres.pdf |
| | \GradWith1stHons\Year 2\Group project\Assessment3\FinalQcards.pdf |

The final group project presentation format is typically the same as that of the interim presentation except it will be longer and therefore require more slides – again your lecturer will inform you of the duration and the number of slides you will need. See 4.2.8.2 Assessment 1: Interim Group Presentation and also 4.2.6 Preparing presentations should you need to recap. Again we will look through the presentation that we gave for the final presentation.

| | |
|---|---|
| Slide1 | is the group project title slide during which we introduced ourselves. |
| Slide2 | this really reintroduces the project and recaps on our design task. Also the opportunity is taken to introduce the M1 to M5 terminology that is used through a number of my slides – this refers to the five robot arm motors. |

| | |
|---|---|
| Slide3 | this recaps on the block segments of our project and how they were divided amongst us. My partner may have spoken throughout this slide and if memory serves I spoke throughout slide 2. |
| Slide4 | begins a run of slides where my partner talks about the VB GUI control program while I remain silent. She explains the purpose of the GUI: that it provides an easy means of controlling the robot arm via the PC and that it sends signals to the decoder interface via the COM port. |
| Slide5 | this slide introduces the Visual Basic programming language and explains why we decided to use it. It also explains that VB is 'event driven' and how this differs from the conventional free running languages (non Windows platforms like earlier BASICs, C and assembler). |
| Slide6 | this slide explains three of the standard methods used in VB which are highly relevant to our GUI program. There are many other methods used within the program but these have been singled out as they are used to initialise the program and send the motor start and stop codes. |
| Slide7 | in this slide the specifics regarding how the COM port is driven in VB is explained. If this is not set up correctly the decoder interface will not see the correct signals and hence the robot arm will not function. |
| Slide8 | explains that we are using a sequence of pulses to specify which motor the decoder interface switches on, and that specific ASC II codes are sent to the interface to dictate the correct control sequences. |
| Slide9 | in this last slide for the GUI the COM port bit rate and accompanying parameters are discussed. It is also explained that the COM signal itself remains static at logic 1 until a sequence is sent, and that this includes a start bit and a stop bit. My decoder interface must interpret these to begin and complete the decoding process. |

| | |
|---|---|
| Slide 10 | in this slide I talk about the second RS232 control code scheme that was used to communicate with the decoder (remember my first scheme failed). |
| Slide 11 | this shows the voltage conditioning circuit, during with I would have explained how it is connected and how it functions, making reference to the five capacitors in the top left table. |
| Slide 12 | this shows the PIC microcontroller segment of my decoder, for which I would have given a talk on every aspect of the circuit. |
| Slide 13 | shows the supply conditioning and decoupling elements of the decoder circuit of which I would probably of spoken on for less than 1 minute since it is a trivial subject compared to that of the decoder itself, but it is also vital. |
| Slide 14 | I show a picture of the RS232 signal as seen from the output side of the voltage conditioning circuit. My talk here would have been a lead into the next slide. |
| Slide 15 | here two subroutines of my decoder program are shown and I give a talk regarding how the positive and negative going edges of the RS232 signal are tracked and thus counted. In actual fact, the key to decoding my transmission scheme is simply to count a number of pulses. |
| Slide 16 | here I show a set of timing calculations and give a talk on various timing/counting aspects of the decoder program. |
| Slide 17 | this follows on from the subject of slide 11, and shows how the decoder auto detects the bit or baud rate and how the microcontroller's timer is used to exit the decode cycle after communication is detected from the RS232 PC COM port. |
| Slide 18 | discusses the flow of two of the decoder program subroutines. Note: I am only talking about these elements of the decoder program, there is not enough time to discuss the whole program (however all the flowcharts in the slideshow represent the key elements of the program). |

| Slide19 | begins a second talk and run of slides for the motor drive segment by my partner. In this slide she explains that her motor drive unit is a repartition of one circuit and the slide depicts a single circuit element which switches a relay to tern the connected motor on and off. All the circuit components are discussed including justifications and selection. |
|---|---|
| Slide20 | in this slide it is explained that an additional relay circuit (same as above) is required to reverse the battery voltage to all motors in order that the motors can spin both clockwise and anticlockwise. This really was a very neat solution on her part to reverse the voltage throughout the circuit. |
| Slide21 | the final slide shows the overall motor drive circuit together with the connection point to my decoder. In comment: I would have included the relay switching wiring to the motors, but this would have been in her report and I doubt it really reflected in the overall mark received. It also may have been cut to stay within the time limit, but my memory does not serve to confirm this. |
| Slide22 | closes the final presentation. At this point a number of questions were asked to both of us, and perhaps more importantly, the lecturers enjoy themselves playing with the PC controlled robot arm. |

It can be seen that this was a well balanced and thorough presentation. Only a small amount of material recaps that of the interim presentation, and more importantly, only so with good reason. The typical reason is planning as it is unlikely that a great deal of ground in terms of implementation will have been addressed before the interim presentation, mainly because of the mechanics of the group element.

The main thing to note is how this presentation (with the inclusion of my partner's slide) tells the 'story' of the whole robot arm interface development. We both succeeded in including the biggest part of the work we carried out – in practice it is more difficult to achieve this in the third year project as it is on a bigger scale. However, that fact serves to demonstrate how important it is to strike a good balance here as experience for that to come.

### 4.2.8.5 Accompanying files for group project.

All assessment files are omitted from this table since their URL paths are given elsewhere in this chapter. Table 9. Accompanying files for group project.

| DIR. | Description | URL path in file structure |
|---|---|---|
| PicSource | The source file from my PIC Decoder assembly program. You may view this in any text editor or Windows Notepad, but you will have to set the open file dialog to 'show all files'.<br><br>If you wish to play with assembling the .asm file or single stepping it in a 'Monitor' you will need MPLAB IDE software from Microchip. http://www.microchip.com/, see MPLAB IDE link on front page. | \GradWith1stHons\Year 2\Groupproject\PicSourse\RobotArm.asm |
| Pictures | Contains the following pictures: | \GradWith1stHons\Year 2\Group project\pictures\ |
| | Group project plan | group_plan.jpg |
| | My overall RS232 Decoder circuit fully built | PH 001.jpg |
| | The robot arm connected to the motor drive circuit board and the decoder. | PH 004.jpg |
| | Close up of same picture, allows you to see the drive motor circuit better. | PH 006.jpg |
| | Circuit diagram of my decoder with the decoding scheme. | Piccct.gif |
| RAcontrol | Contains files from my test PC GUI program, including an executable and VB source project. One again, you will need a suitable installation as mentioned above. | \GradWith1stHons\Year 2\Group project\RAcontrol\RAsender.exe<br><br>and<br><br>\GradWith1stHons\Year 2\Group project\RAcontrol\RAsender.vbp |

**Table 9. Accompanying files for group project.**

### 4.2.9 Major Project (third year)

*4.2.9.1 Overview*

Your Major Project is the single most important component of your studies, for example, in my degree this project had the same weighting as three academic modules. The weighting of your major project may vary depending on the subject/classification of your degree and you will be made aware of its weighting when you begin the project module. Once again, I can only relate my experience in order to advise you with the major project, but it is likely it will play out as follows.

You will be given a Major Project Handbook and a number of projects to choose from. You are also likely to be able to suggest a project of your own, but this would need to be negotiated with the members of the project supervisory team. As such it may be rejected or a compromise may be agreed if the suggested project is deemed to complex or not complex enough. Thus aspects of your suggestion may be removed or if the suggestion is insufficient in some way a member of the supervisory team may suggest extra elements to make your suggestion viable as a major project. Let's begin by taking a look at my project handbook followed by the Project Proposal which outlines the project I chose.

Before that it seems fitting to introduce my project here. My task was to build two digital filters (for filtering sampled digitised audio); one was a novel design that was believed to have certain power saving properties, the other a typical design used throughout industry – the kind used in typical household appliances like your HiFi or TV. The aim was to prove the low power version worked and saved power, or even disprove the power saving argument. After all, the jury is always out till there's a verdict.

## 4.2.9.2 Major Project Handbook

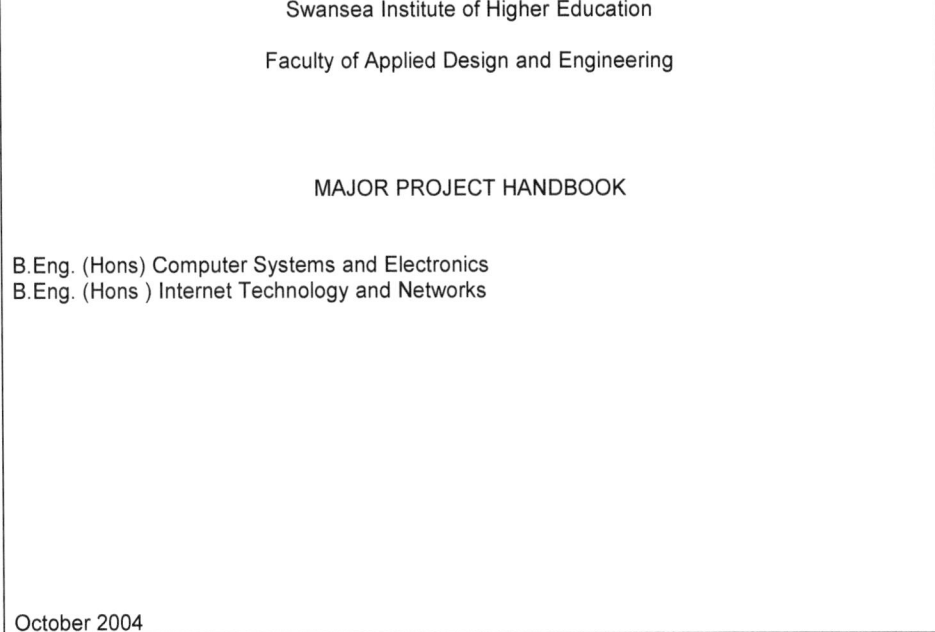

Table 10. Front page of Major Project Handbook

## Introduction

Major Project is an important component of your studies. In terms of its contribution to the final award, it must be noted that it has the same weighting as three academic modules, and has a significant effect on the classification of the award. Therefore it is vital that the student demonstrates a responsible attitude in all aspects of the Major Project execution. The student is reminded of the Quality Assurance Agency framework for higher education qualifications, and the descriptors for a qualification for Bachelors degree with Honours.

*Honours degrees are awarded to students who have demonstrated:*

1. *a systematic understanding of key aspects of the field of study, including acquisition of coherent and detailed knowledge.*

2. *an ability to deploy accurately, established techniques of analysis and enquiry.*

3. *conceptual understanding that enables the student:*

    *to devise and sustain arguments, and/or to solve problems, using ideas and techniques, some of which are at the forefront of a discipline.*

    *to describe and comment upon particular aspects of current research, or equivalent advanced scholarship.*

4. *an appreciation of the uncertainty, ambiguity and limits of knowledge.*

5. *the ability to manage their own learning, and to make use of scholarly reviews and primary sources.*

The student is advised to reflect on the above points since they represent the primary objectives of the Major Project, and act as guidelines for determining the criteria for assessment.

## Major Project Assessment

The assessment of the Major Project considers four separate aspects. These are listed along with their corresponding assessment weightings:

| | |
|---|---|
| Project Feasibility Study report | 5% |
| Interim viva voce | 15% |
| Final viva voce | 35% |
| Major Project report | 40% |
| Exhibition | 5% |

## Table 11. Page 2 of Major Project Handbook

The student is expected to pass each of the above in order to satisfactorily complete the Major Project.

The tasks, upon which the assessments will be made, reflect the overall project execution, and the student must consider:

1. A realistic project management strategy
2. A clear process of design synthesis
3. Construction and testing capability
4. Technical report writing
5. Self evaluation and critique

Irrespective of the nature of the project, it is ability of the student undertaking the above tasks, and the relationship to the qualification descriptors, that determine the assessment grading.

**Project Proposal**

The choice of a suitable project will be evolved by a process of negotiation, between the student and members of the project supervisory team. A list of project titles may be made available from members of academic staff. Such titles will often reflect an interest or relate to areas of specialised research. The student is encouraged to identify a project, in the belief that ownership is better placed with the student. When the final choice is made, a Project Proposal must be completed and subsequently approved by the Major Project Coordinator. The student will be provided with the appropriate form and must complete all headings:

Name
Programme
Academic Project Supervisor
Industrial Project Supervisor (if appropriate for part time students)
Project Description
Signatories (Project Coordinator AND student)

Once completed, this confirms a commitment by the student to undertaking a project according to the agreed title. A request for a change of title at any future time must be made formally to the Project Supervisory Team, which will review the specific circumstances. The Project Coordinator will provide the appropriate application form.

**Table 12. Page 3 of Major Project Handbook**

**Feasibility Report**

Having made a choice of project title, the student is expected to produce a feasibility study report. This is a detailed document, which identifies the following:

   Name
   Project Title
   Programme of Study
   Introduction
   Project Objectives
   Preliminary Research
   Project Plan
   Resources and Materials

This report defines what achievements are expected. The student must give due consideration to defining realistic timescales to specific tasks, and to recognise the resources needed. The objectives must be carefully thought out, and must show the character and scope of the project, in a clear and unambiguous manner. This report will be regarded as a properly structured technical report with properly annotated diagrams, referenced text, references and bibliography, Gantt charts etc. The report is likely to be of approximately 2000 word length.

**Major Project Supervision**

A team of academic staff constitutes the project supervisory team. The student will be allocated a named project supervisor, but can draw on the broader experience of the team when assistance is required. The supervisor will no doubt have specialist knowledge to guide with technical issues, however most problems arise from project management complications or some general technical issue that can be resolved by other team members. The supervision team will also undertake assessment. Both viva voce will be assessed by a team subset, and the project report will be second marked.

Any concerns about supervision, and any appeals against the nature of assessment must initially be made via the Project Coordinator. If the student remains dissatisfied, then the student has the right of appeal both at Faculty and Institute level. The student may write formally to the Dean of Faculty stating such grievances.

**Interim Viva Voce**

This represents a midpoint in the timescale of the project execution. At this stage, the student is expected to have completed the 'design' stage of the project. The student is allocated 1 5minutes to make an oral presentation, and followed immediately by a 10 minute questioning session. Consideration will have been given to:

## Table 13. Page 4 of Major Project Handbook

|  |
|---|
| Alternative design approaches |
| Thoroughness of literature reviews |
| Recognising the key issues of the project |
| Small-scale experimental activities |
| Production of general arrangement drawings |
| Time management issues |
| The student will produce overhead project slides (preferably using Microsoft PowerPoint) for use on an overhead projector unit. Should the student require the use of digital projection, it is the responsibility of the student to complete the necessary booking form and submit this to the Faculty AV Technician staff, and confirm availability. No responsibility will be taken by the supervision team for software incompatibility, non-availability of digital projection equipment (other than a overhead projector) or any problems that may prevent the student making a presentation, at the published time and place. Two members of the supervision team will assess the interim viva voce. |
| **Final Viva Voce** |
| The theme of this presentation is 'analysis and evaluation'. Similar to the interim presentation, the student is allocated 15 minutes, but can expect a more rigorous questioning session from three assessors. The student will be expected to produce a professional presentation, clearly showing that lessons have been learnt from the previous experience. The student will be expected to demonstrate: |
| Use of modelling and simulation methods to test designs |
| Show experimental results |
| Demonstrate an analysis of experimental results |
| Professional response to questioning |
| Critical appraisal of the time management of the project |
| Critical appraisal of the outcomes measured against the feasibility study benchmark |

**Table 14. Page 5 of Major Project Handbook**

**Major Project Report**

The report represents the largest contribution to the project grade. It is important to note that a good report is the outcome of a well-executed project, and must not be regarded as an opportunity to make good, a generally poor performance. The report is a formal document, produced to a standardised presentation, and will set Out all aspects of the project activity. The production of the report will generally commence around the Easter holiday, so leaving sufficient time prior to the mid-May submission date. Example reports will be made available for inspection at the appropriate time. Guidance notes on the production of the report are enclosed.

**Exhibition**

The purpose of the exhibition is to give the student the opportunity to demonstrate the functionality of the project. It is likely that electronic hardware, or software has been developed, and this work will have formed the basis of presentations, together with the content of the report. It is recognised that the time allocated to the final viva voce is not sufficient to enable a detailed examination of the 'end product'. The student will produce a display board presentation, and show all aspects of hardware/software as appropriate. This is an opportunity for the External Examiner to be present, and will, if appropriate, provide a forum to interview the student specifically about the project, or in more general terms.

**Logbook**

The student is required to supply an A4 size hard covered textbook. This will contain a record of all project activities. It is intended to be a notebook, in which all ideas, research notes etc are recorded. Do not remove pages and clearly date each entry.

Members of the supervisory-team will interview the student, from time to time, and it is the responsibility of the student to make the logbook available at such times. At the conclusion of the interview, the supervisor will sign the logbook as evidence of the interview and include comments reflecting the outcome of the interview.

**Communication**

All timetables of assessment, and any relevant information regarding communication to the student will be displayed on the notice board, adjacent to room MBG03. It is the responsibility of the student to make note of such information.

**Table 15. Page 6 of Major Project Handbook**

### Major Project Assessment Timetable (2004/05)

| | |
|---|---|
| Identification of Project Specification | - 15-10-04 |
| Submission of feasibility study | - 29-10-04 |
| Interim viva | - late Nov/early Dec |
| Submission of Major Project Report | - 1st/2$^{nd}$ week May |
| Final viva | - 2$^{nd}$/3$^{rd}$ May |
| Exhibition | early June |

Note: The Major Project exhibition will coincide with a visit by the External Examiner, immediately prior to the Examining Board for the programme.

**Supervisory Team**

The following staff are on the supervisory team for the Major Project:

- Dr Ian Wells
- Mike Vanstone
- Gaynor Thomas
- Gwynfor Higgins

Please make an appointment to see a member of staff at a mutually convenient time.

**Materials**

Each student is allocated £100 for the procurement of materials for the project. The student is responsible for identifying the necessary items and completing and order form. The order form is available from Mr Tim Griffin-Thomas.

If electronic components are required, check availability from the Electronic Stores, first referring to the stores catalogue supplied. On identification of components, complete the appropriate stores requisition form. Datasheets and other useful software are available on CD format. The student is expected to supply a blank recordable CD for this purpose, to the Stores Technician.

**Table 16. Page 7 of Major Project Handbook**

**Plagiarism**

Plagiarism is an extremely serious offence and is dealt with severely. Plagiarism is an attempt to present work which is not yours. It includes research material which is presented without acknowledgement of the author. It may be text, diagrams, images, extracts from books, internet websites, journals and magazines; irrespective of whether this material has been published or not. Also note that anyone allowing their work to be copied is equally as guilty. There is absolutely no excuse for plagiarising work, and it is your responsibility to correctly reference your source material.

Should you be accused of plagiarism, the following actions can be implemented:

The student will be informed in writing to state clearly the reasons for the accusation. This will be undertaken by the member of staff concerned. The student will also be initially interviewed and a written report of the meeting will be sent to the Head of School.

The Dean of Faculty will consider the circumstances, and will invite a response from the student. If the Dean of Faculty considers the accusation to be justified then formal disciplinary proceedings will be auctioned, and the matter will be placed before a University of Wales, Standing Panel of Enquiry of Senate.

If the panel concludes that a case against the student is justified, certain penalties will be considered.

- A formal warning
- A reduced mark for a piece of work
- A requirement for the work to be repeated
- Exclusion from examinations in that session
- Exclusion from the University.

*There is a simple way to avoid this happening to you............*

*properly reference your source material*

## Table 17. Page 8 of Major Project Handbook

| | |
|---|---|
| Module Title: | Major Project |
| Date Of Validation: | |
| Module Number | M3X6839 |
| Module Value: | 40 credits |
| Level: | 3 |
| Faculty Responsible for Delivery: | Faculty of Applied Design and Engineering |
| Prerequisites: | All Year 1 and Year 2 Modules |

AIMS:

1. To develop the innovative and creative skills of the student within the field of the engineering specialism being studied.
2. To encourage and develop self-motivation and investigative ability.

OUTCOME STATEMENTS:

Upon the successful completion of this module the student will be able to demonstrate:

1. Identification of a problem within the chosen engineering specialism.
2. Application of an appropriate research methodology for the problem
3. Generation of a project plan.
4. Application of appropriate skills to the solution of the engineering problem.
5. Critical appraisal of the results of the investigation.
6. Communication in visual, written and oral forms of the results of the project investigation.

INDICATIVE CONTENT:

Students will undertake projects which will be innovative, academically demanding and which will require a sound theoretical knowledge. They will be expected to work with the minimum of direct supervision in the process leading to the solution of the identified problem.

Students will be expected to acquire new knowledge mainly based on concepts previously taught in supporting modules. Issues raised in earlier modules (particularly Group Project), e.g. costings, project planning, research methodology, ethics, will be developed as appropriate.

The project may be formulated through a variety of means - student idea, industrial liaison, staff-student discussion, or a combination of these means. Although the ultimate choice of project to be undertaken rests with the student, that choice will not be made without consultation with the Project Director. The identification of the problem to be investigated will ideally be made by the end of level 2 of the programme.

The normal progression for the execution of the Major Project, for full time students, will be as follows:

**Table 18. Page 9 of Major Project Handbook**

| | | |
|---|---|---|
| Stage 1 | - | This is a preliminary outline of the proposed project to allow project viability to be assessed and will be submitted by mid-October. |
| Stage 2 | - | For this, the preparation and planning stage, the student will research the background to the identified problem by the means most appropriate literature survey and analysis, market analysis, industrial contact etc. Methods of problem solution will be formulated and evaluated. Areas requiring more in-depth background knowledge will be studied at this stage. A time and resource requirements project plan will also be formulated. |
| | | This stage should he completed by December of the 1st Semester, when an oral examination will be given (see 'Assessment'). |
| Stage 3 | - | Presentation of the results of the project in the form of:<br>(i)   A written report<br>(ii)  An oral examination<br>(iii) Visual display summarising the project e.g. PowerPoint presentation<br>This stage will be completed by May of the final year. |

For part time students the above time scales will be adjusted accordingly.

TEACHING AND LEARNING STRATEGY:

| | Hours |
|---|---|
| Tutorials | 30 |
| Student Private Study | 370 |
| TOTAL | 400 |

IMPLEMENTATION:

The student will essentially be working independently. To assist the student an appropriate team of project advisors drawn from the teaching staff will be formed. Members of the team will be available at known times throughout the working week to answer queries that each student may have. At all times it is the intention of the advisors to guide the student to his/her own solution of the problem(s). Consensus marking of all oral examinations, reports and exhibits will be carried out by the team. The written report is double marked. The Project Director will chair the meetings of the team when assessment is discussed and finalised. In the event of an unresolved disagreement about an assessment the external examiner will be asked to arbitrate.

Throughout each assessment stage the assessment team will be seeking evidence that the student has applied the knowledge gained from the programme in an accurate and coherent fashion, and is able to show flair, creativity and investigative ability, with the necessary communication skills that this implies, to the solution of the problem identified.

If a significant deviation from the original project plan is necessary, then clear evidence for the rationale of the change and its consequences must be obtained during the later stage of the assessment. Any changes of this nature will be the subject of critical evaluation by the assessment team, and must be justified in the final viva.

**Table 19. Page 10 of Major Project Handbook**

## ASSESSMENT

Assessment will be as follows:

| Stage | Date | Topic | Mode of Assessment | Mark (%) |
|---|---|---|---|---|
| 1 | October | Initial Report | Report | 5 |
| 2 | December | Preparation & Planning | Interim Viva | 15 |
| 3 | May | Conclusions | Viva | 40 |
|   |   |   | Written Report | 35 |
|   |   |   | Exhibition | 5 |

| Stage | |
|---|---|
| 1 | Project proposal: initial literature and market survey, recognition of scope of work involved, project viability. |
| 2 | Research and project plan: literature/market analysis, conclusions from specialist discussions, personal insight, feasibility of the solution and plan, written report and log book, communication skills. |
| 3 | Viva:   Technical knowledge; Clarity and appropriate level of presentation. Product: innovation, creativity, originality; Level of technical implementation.<br><br>Written report: structure, clarity and content. Product analysis and evaluation; Evidence of background research and investigative ability;<br><br>Exhibition: appropriateness and quality. |

## READING LIST:

As appropriate to the project.

## PHYSICAL RESOURCES:

- Equipment and consumables appropriate to specific projects

## ROOM REQUIREMENTS:

- Laboratories and workshops appropriate to specific projects.

## STAFF RESOURCES:

Project supervisory team
- Dr. I Wells
- M. Vanstone
- G. Thomas
- P. Kear

**Table 20. Page 11 of Major Project Handbook**

**PROJECT REPORT FORMAT**

1) PROJECT REPORTS

In the past, project submissions have on occasion done less than justice to the work undertaken. The objective is clearly to indicate the worth of the investigation itself in its reading, research and quality of investigation methods, as well as issues involving the task in hand. Clear links are sought between the results analysis, conclusions, recommendations and implementation plans. Each should build on the previous stage of argument. If the structure and content of the report fail to show these substantiating links, then no matter how brilliant, innovative or acceptable the recommendations, the project submission will itself be borderline or worse in its assessment.

The aim of the project report is to convince your supervisors and organisational audience that:

- the stated objectives of your project make sense in context.

- the methodology of the investigation was chosen well and that you are critically aware of any inherent flaws and the effects of divergences from your plan. Additionally, that you know and
- show the strength or weakness of the evidence on which you base your recommendations.

- well chosen sources have been used and a good depth of reading has been undertaken, and identifiably used in your investigation.(Sources must be referenced within the text).

You must agree a detailed draft structure of the report with your project coordinator generally within the following outline. This is to achieve the consistency between projects, which is desired by your supervisory team and external examiners. Adaptations of the structure may prove necessary but should be kept to a minimum, and have your project coordinator supervisors' agreement.

2) THE PRESENTATION OF PROJECT REPORTS

**Table 21. Page 12 of Major Project Handbook**

| | | |
|---|---|---|
| 2.1) | | Each student submitting a project report must present TWO copies in the following manner:<br>The copies, which may be the original and a carbon or Xerox copy of the original, must be presented in a bound form, with standard covers. (Swansea Institute window covers). The form of binding may be either plastic ring binders or plastic spines; no other form of binding will be accepted.<br>TWO copies of the report must be submitted in accordance with the Institute regulations, with the project coordinator reserving the right to request a third copy. The report must be prepared on A4 size white paper of a minimum weight of 80g/m2, in accordance with the following specifications: |
| | a) | The text must be typed on one side of the paper only, with margins of not less that 3 cm on all four sides. |
| | b) | Only mathematical text may be hand-written and must be spaced out; superscripts and subscripts must be clearly shown as such. |
| | c) | The pages of text, including inserted illustrations and appendices, must be numbered consecutively at the bottom centre of each page. |
| | d) | Photographs, drawings, graphs and other illustrations which are not incorporated in the text must be reproduced on A4 size card (not heavier than 230g!m2), leaving a margin of not less that 2 cm all round. Where large-scale engineering drawings are used, copies reduced to A4 size must be included in the report where appropriate. In any case, a complete set of the original drawings should be saved onto CD and included at the rear of the report. |
| 2.2) | | |
| | a) | The cover (displayed in cover window) must contain, in this order:<br>the name of the author<br>the title of the work<br>the award for which the project is submitted |
| | b) | The title page (Appendix A) must contain, in this order:<br>the name of the Institute<br>the Division of specialisation<br>the award for which the project is submitted(e.g. BEng, or MEng)<br>the academic year of original submission<br>the name of the author<br>the title<br>the names of the supervisory team<br>the date of presentation |
| A statement shall be included at the foot of the title page of all Degree projects which will state that 'This project is submitted in partial submission for the degree concerned.' | | |

**Table 22. Page 13 of Major Project Handbook**

> 2.3) The page or pages immediately following the title page must contain an abstract of not more than 300 words.
>
> 3) **REPORT FORMAT**
>
> It is suggested that the physical arrangements of each report should be as follows:
> - a) Front Cover (Reference 2.2a)
> - b) Title Page (Reference 2.2b)
> - c) Abstract (max. 300 words only)
> - d) List of Contents
> - e) List of Figures
> - f) Notation
> - g) Main body of text
> - h) References and/or Bibliography
> - i) Appendices
> - j) Tables, unless these are included in the text
> - k) Illustrations, unless these are included in the text
> - l) Back Cover with attached CD if required
>
> **Title Page**
>
> The title page must contain the various items as listed in section 2.2b. A suitable layout is shown in Appendix A. It is not customary to include military ranks, degrees or professional qualifications.
>
> **List of Contents**
>
> This should be entitled 'CONTENTS' and is a statement of the main headings under which the text of the report is arranged. Page numbers should be those on which sections start and it is suggested that inclusive numbering, e.g. '22-23' is not used. In the 'CONTENTS' the section titles listed should appear in the same type size-as used to designate them in the text, i.e. Upper Case for main headings, Lower Case for subheadings. Where there are more than five illustrations, a list of figures should be included. This will be entitled 'FIGURES'. Figure titles in this list should not be in capitals and the word 'Figure' should not be repeated each time.
>
> Both the 'CONTENTS' and 'FIGURES' should begin on an unnumbered page. If the contents list is a short one, e.g. half a page, the list of figures may begin below it.
>
> **Notation**
>
> Any symbols used in the report are to be listed under the heading 'NOTATION' and should appear before the main text, again on an unnumbered page.

**Table 23. Page 14 of Major Project Handbook**

> **Main Text**
>
> THE TEXT OF YOUR REPORT MAY BE TYPED IN SINGLE 1.5 OR DOUBLE SPACING AND IN THE STYLE PRESCRIBED IN THE REGULATIONS. THAT IS, IT MUST BE TYPED ON ONE SIDE OF THE PAPER ONLY ON A4 PAPER WITH THE APPROPRIATE MARGINS, BEAR IN MIND THAT, SHOULD YOU CHOOSE TO HAVE YOUR REPORT TYPED IN 1.5 OR DOUBLE SPACING, IT WILL INCREASE YOUR COSTS SO FAR AS TYPING AND PHOTOCOPYING ARE CONCERNED.
> PAGE NUMBERING SHOULD COMMENCE WITH THE INTRODUCTION ON PAGE 1 AND SHOULD INCLUDE INSERTED ILLUSTRATIONS. IT IS SUGGESTED THAT PAGE NUMBERS SHOULD BE CONSECUTIVE AND APPEAR AT THE BOTTOM CENTRE OF EACH SHEET. THERE IS NO NEED TO WRITE 'PAGE' BEFORE EACH NUMBER.
>
> The main text should begin with the Introduction, which should deal with the background to the work, and any reasons for undertaking it, and references to any other work done on the subject.
>
> It is not possible to produce any hard and fast rules for the arrangement of the main text, since the variety of subjects treated in projects is so wide and each has it own conventions and methods of approach. In general, however, students are reminded that clear details of any theoretical models or equipment used should be included, as should any techniques or procedures involved, and that a clear and logical presentation is a help to all using the project, whether as assessor or subsequent reader.
>
> Following on the main text, any conclusions reached from the work should be presented, preferably in an itemised form. Recommendations may be included at this stage.
>
> **References/Bibliography**
>
> After the conclusion and recommendations, any assistance given is then to be acknowledged and followed by a list of the' works referred to in the text. The suggested method of listing references is shown below:
>
> **References**
>
> The following conventions should be used:
>
> **Books:**  Reference number
>   Authors'-or editors' name(s) plus initials (Capitals)
>   Year of Publication (in brackets)
>   Title of book (underlined)
>   Publisher

**Table 24. Page 15 of Major Project Handbook**

| |
|---|
| e.g.:    1    SMITH, G T (1993) <u>CNC Machining</u> Springer Verlag, England<br><br>         2    HADLEY, G (1992) Linear Programming Addison-Wesley, Massachusetts<br><br>Journal Articles:      Reference number<br>                           Authors name(s) plus initials (capitals)<br>                           Year of publication (in brackets)<br>                           Title of article<br>                           Journal (underlined)<br>                           Volume<br>                           Number<br>                           Page numbers<br><br>e.g.:    3    MOLE, RH (1990) Dynamic optimisation of vehicle fleet size.<br><br>           <u>Operational Research Quarterly</u> 26, 1, 25-34<br><br>        4    THOMPSON, F P (1991) Statistics and the environment — the third London Airport Study. <u>The Statistician</u> XXI, 1, 19-30.<br><br>**Speeches, newspaper articles, proceedings, internet articles, e-mails etc.**<br><br>These should be in the spirit of the above.<br><br>**Bibliography**<br><br>The Bibliography should be arranged in alphabetical order of authors/editors. It should be placed immediately before any appendices.<br><br>**Appendices**<br><br>Appendices are more detailed explanations of items in the text which, it is felt, require rather more attention than could be given in the main body of the text. Appendices should be lettered A, B, C.<br><br>The reader/audience for this report is your supervisor and an informed member of the organisation whom you wish to influence. They are looking at the data, its analysis and the quality of the argument and substantiation of your conclusions and recommendations. They are also looking to see that your recommendations are practical and that due account is taken of any challenges in implementation.<br><br>Attention should be paid to the overall linkage of material, one device for which is a chapter summary, signposting and link passages. A reader is helped by each stage being introduced and summarised so that the flow of the overall argument is emphasised. This is difficult to achieve when the draft is produced slowly over several weeks. You are advised to read you draft as a whole, through the eyes of a non-expert to ensure that such linkages are obvious. |

**Table 25. Page 16 of Major Project Handbook**

> Your reader will wish to be able to cross-reference from section to section to follow arguments or re-develop them themselves from the data provided. A decimal numbering system of sections and diagrams, etc. is thus required.
>
> PLEASE REMEMBER THAT YOUR READER HAS LIMITED TIME TO CONSIDER YOUR OPUS. REMEMBER THAT APPENDICES ARE A DEVICE TO REMOVE DETAIL FROM THE MAIN TEXT.
>
> **Proof Reading**
>
> CAREFUL proofreading is ultimately YOUR responsibility.

**Table 26. Page 17 of Major Project Handbook**

As you can see, the criteria for the Major Project is both strict and drawn out. There is no real need to analyse this handbook as you have gained good experience from the Group Project in year two. Just be sure you follow the criteria you receive from your university closely and present a good project. Once again, when you have agreed a project plan with your project supervisor be sure to stick to it and don't let yourself full behind.

Remember, with the project being leveraged at a weighting of two to three modules you cannot afford the loss of marks on this subject. To ensure a First overall you really need to aim for a First in this project unit too. The examples provided in this chapter are good examples in terms of detail, depth and length, so be sure to maintain a parallel standard and you should get the marks you need.

### *4.2.9.3 Project Proposal*

| Coursework Example for this section. | |
|---|---|
| Path: | \GradWith1stHons\Year 3\Major Project\Project Proposal\Project Proposal.pdf |

Once you have chosen a project your supervisor is likely to ask you to produce a short document called a Project Proposal, outlining the project itself and the resources you will need to complete the project. This is not an assessment so there are no marks and the format is really very simple.

You can see my Project Proposal by following the URL path above.

### *4.2.9.4 Assessment 1: Project Feasibility Study Report*

| Coursework Example for this section. | |
|---|---|
| Path: | \GradWith1stHons\Year 3\Major Project\Assessment1\FeasibilityReport.pdf |

As the title suggests, in assessment one the student has to explore the feasibility of their project as a practical exercise. This is the type of document a designer (of some description) might have to submit to his (or her) manager to OK a given design, making sure it isn't going to exceed budget, only the criteria is somewhat different being a university project. Of course the other difference is: you already know your project is feasible otherwise your supervisor would not have approved it where as in industry (for example) a designer would often submit an equivalent document without knowing if his manager would OK it.

In my case, and yours is likely to be similar, the report must introduce the technology, the project itself, how the project is to be constructed, the project objectives, research to be considered, the project plan, test breakdown, resources needed and a conclusion. Now is probably a good time to share some good news: with the Major Project you get one-to-one tuition with a project supervisor. He or she will tell you exactly what is expected in this document (and the others); all you have to do is interpret the information correctly and get on with the work.

Because of the sheer size of the Major Project workload (that's the bad news in case you were waiting for it) I am not going to make detailed dissections of all my work. It would take too much space and I think after surviving the group project and other assessments throughout year two you are in a strong position to be able to read my work and assess the required standard yourself. Pretty much every detail I went into on the 4.2.8 Group Project (second year) holds true, there is just a lot more work to address here than before.

Actually, there really isn't much more to say about this one, other than it is comparable to a small assignment. Naturally my tips on writing assignments and reports are equally applicable here and throughout the rest of the major project except when overridden by the 4.2.9.2 Major Project Handbook, so do be careful as YOUR (not the one I have included) handbook is your first port of call when considering report formats and styles etc.

### 4.2.9.5 Assessment 2: Interim Viva Voce

| Coursework Example for this section. | |
| --- | --- |
| Path: | GradWith1stHons\Year 3\Major Project\Assessment2\IntrimVivaPres.pdf |

The interim presentation is similar to that of its counterpart in the year two group project in that it evolves around the same elements, but there are two differences; it is a personal presentation you will make on your own and it is twice the length. These are the only differences so when planning your interim presentation you should consult 4.2.6.1 How to plan an Interim Presentation and apply this guide to your Major Project. For now let's take a look at my presentation (file path is above) to see how it meets the criteria discussed in 4.2.6.1.

| Slide1 | my interim presentation begins with a cover page as normal – you shouldn't pay too much attention to the picture cover, as it wasn't a requirement. |
|---|---|
| Slide2 and 3 | are two pages of solid introduction so the lecturers (there is likely to be more than just your supervisor present) get a real feel for the work that will be produced in hardware throughout the project and the goals to be achieved. |
| Slide4 | is a talk through the filter design in MATLAB. The two filters are to have the same properties; that is the same input signal could be applied to both and the output signal should be exactly the same. So although this slide depicts a design process it is more a question of simulating a number of filters and then choosing a good example to work with throughout the project, and that was the premise of the verbal content. |
| Slide5 | explains how digital filters work and gives the coefficient fractions (the coefficients are a list of numbers that when applied to the filter input by means of Finite Impulse Response (FIR) filter mathematics will produce the resulting output) for the filter designed in the previous slide. The coefficients are then plotted to show the filter's response function. |
| Slide6 | is a block representation of how digital filters work, although it is very much cut down as only five coefficient multipliers are shown. With regard to the talk, I am gearing up the verbal content to begin explaining how hardware in the low power Primitive Operator Filter (POF) differs from the conventional design, and how and why it should save power (which could be equated to battery life for example). Which of course is the whole premise of my project. |

| | |
|---|---|
| Slide7 | this slide presents a number of important points of information and ties them to an example. This allows the verbal content to compare and contrast the low power POF design with the conventional design. The next slide follows on from this – so these are two important sides that not only provide good marks but also serve to pave the way for more important content. |
| Slide8 | shows a block diagram of the POF filter, with a blow up of the interconnection of the integrated circuit BUS pins which are responsible for multiplying the inputs with the coefficients in conjunction with the adders, depicted by '(+)'. The verbal content here would be explaining how the POF filter is operating with specific respect to the hardware components. |
| Slide9 | here four filter designs are being compared (with regard to window classification) in MATLAB once more. This is really a justification slide and talk as there are several different filter designs that could have been chosen to build, but my choice has to be verbally justified in terms of best all round specification. This insures more good marks as it was vital to choose a good example and a fair amount of time was spent on this. |
| Slide10, 11, 12, 13 and 14 | these slides examine the merits of different filter resolution and justify both my chosen 'resolution' and filter window design whilst displaying and verbally contrasting the various coefficient permutations with respect to design. The red numbers represent 'single coefficient' values in that there is only one physical hardware representation of that number. Filter resolution is something that cannot be explained in the confines of this space but it is discussed in my project report. |

| | |
|---|---|
| Slide15 | shows the delay line for a 8 bit (the resolution) Hamming window filter design. My design was 10 bit, but the 8 bit delay line is specifically chosen to show that more coefficients are converted to zero when a low resolution is applied. This is demonstrated by the delay elements missing adder blocks and inputs in between, circled in blue. For example a 10 bit resolution would have far less uninterrupted runs of delay elements (therefore far less zeros). |
| Slide16 | here the quantisation error is examined and discussed with respect to a window plot. There is an error introduced into the filter as a result of applying a resolution (the raw line shown in red has no error because it is not subject to a resolution). Unfortunately this error cannot be avoided as a hardware implementation of any filter has to have a resolution to work within – one can only increase resolution to improve on error and this reflects the verbal content of this slide. |
| Slide17 | is the first time a block representation of the chosen filter to be designed in hardware (or built – both terms are correct as an element of hardware design is needed to overcome a number of problems) is actually shown. Verbally I would be explaining specific detail to this filter design, i.e. pointing out that the adder blocks (+) with black numbers are being summed to make those with red numbers and further pointing out that the adder block outputs feed into a delay line similar to that seen already. |
| Slide18 | this slide displays the project plan or schedule as a Gant chart, and the verbal content would be providing various explanations around this display. This of course is the forecasting element which exists in all interim presentations and is discussed in 4.2.6.1 How to plan an Interim Presentation. |

The remaining two slides are simply a conclusion and end slide; you can see my conclusion is really just a recap of what has happed and a forecast as to what should happen if everything goes to plan, hence omission of the last two slides. After comparing my commentary of these slides to the slides themselves you should be able to appreciate that this was a very thorough presentation and yet it ran very much to time – both those elements will be instrumental in gaining you high marks in your interim presentation.

### 4.2.9.6 Assessment 3: Final Viva Voce

| Coursework Example for this section. | |
|---|---|
| Path: | \GradWith1stHons\Year 3\Major Project\Assessment3\FinalViva.pdf |

Being the final presentation it carries a lot more marks than the interim and it is likely the project supervisor will be fairly rigorous about what materials you are expect to include. Usually a strong element of theory regarding whatever it is you are working on is required, so be sure you are clear on what's expected before you plan the presentation.

It could well be similar in format to mine as I was told to include a couple of slides on FRI Filter theory before going into the depths of my project. The format and tips discussed in 4.2.6.2 How to plan a Final Presentation are also very relevant so do consult them when planning your presentation. Let's take a look at my presentation; once again we will do this with a close description of the presentation.

| Slide1 | this time you may notice that the project title has become elongated; this change was made to more closely represent the work I was researching and testing in the project. |
|---|---|

Slides continue overleaf:

| Slide2 & 3 | these two introduction slides begin by simply stating the purpose of the project and then the process for testing the theory of the project (remember my project is about proving or disproving a theory). However before the theory can be tested a considerable amount of hardware has to be constructed, so this process is outlined up to the testing phase in the introduction. This is important: in the space of two slides the project has been almost completely summarised, thus I am in a strong position to get technical, but the introduction stops short of revealing tests and results. Unless told otherwise, this would be a good format to follow – this viva is worth high marks so it's worth maximising your impression. Almost certainly at least one lecturer who knows nothing of your project will be present, so even if your supervisor is won over by your effort it is still important to impress the newcomer. |
|---|---|
| Slide4 to 8 | the next five slides are spent discussing FIR theory – as this is a technically deep topic, it begins gently for slide three and then the theory ramps up a notch or two. If your subject is technically deep try and keep it in layman's terms where possible, there isn't a great deal of point in getting very technical as you should have proven yourself to your supervisor and also, it is better to address your project evenly during the time you have. Another thing to remember with theory is to link the theory to the relevant aspects of your project, in this presentation this was achieved in slides 6, 7 and 9. Also keep in mind: your supervisor may choose to ask you a question regarding the theory section that pushes deeper than your explanation, so you better know your subject and be able to anticipate likely questions. If you simplify the theory there are a number of benefits: you are not explaining in highly technical terms that could trip you up in a presentation environment, you are likely to make better use of time, you are leaving room for questions and you are respecting the understanding of newcomers sitting in. |

| | |
|---|---|
| Slide 9 | is basically a recap of slide 8 in the interim presentation with more verbal technical depth as the circular overlay is now applied to my filter and not a pictorial example. There is good reason for the placement of this slide: it serves as a pre-cursor to the introduction of a technical problem that had to be overcome in the design. Incidentally, recapping on sides from the Interim Viva is good practice providing you don't over do it and that you are able to add more depth where applicable – I recapped on three slides and given that I have a total of twenty, this is probably a good ratio. |
| Slide 10 & 11 | in these two slides the problem that must be overcome in hardware is introduced. Actually there are two problems but they both have a common narrative – that is, my filter does not support negative input samples, nor does it support negative coefficient numbers. Both of these elements must be accounted for if the filter is to function correctly. In slide 11 I would also have moved from the problem to the mathematical solution in verbal discourse. |
| Slide 12 | explains my hardware implantation of the mathematical solution as a single block diagram. That is, it would have been explained that a repetition of these blocks is needed throughout the filter design. |
| Slide 13 to 15 | explains another aspect of the project that was being experimented with: a computer program that actually produces filter hardware VHDL source code ready for synthesis. I did not have to pursue this aspect; it was more of a personal interest brought about by being a programmer. Actually, this really impressed the project supervisor and may have been a measure of encouragement to lavish me with good marks, but this was never an intention. |
| Slide 16 & 17 | these two slides are a pre-cursor to the conclusion (as is slide 18) in that you cannot conclude until you have presented the results of the project testing or 'trials' to prove that the project does what you set out to achieve – providing that the project is complete that is. In sixteen the test set up for both filters is shown (both setups are identical) and in seventeen a short snapshot of test results is presented. |

| | |
|---|---|
| Slide 18 | is a recap of the project plan from the Interim Viva and simply states that on the whole the project went as scheduled which always looks impressive as it demonstrates good planning from the outset. If your project goes off the rails, remember to positively justify it as discussed in 4.2.6.2 How to plan a Final Presentation. |
| Slide 19 | is the conclusion, which in my case also provides an explanation of what may of – in theory – hampered my testing as the results were not as conclusive as my supervisor and I had hoped. This quite rightly was worthy of some explanation. |

Once again it can be seen that this was a well balanced and thorough presentation. In a way the chosen content was a good compromise as only a small amount of material recaps that of the interim presentation. So if you were to put the presentations side by side you would have a complete 'story' of the project. Which of course is how it should be as a fair amount of work has been carried out before the interim presentation, but you don't want to go over that a second time unless there is good reason to. The best reason to recap is when doing so sets up the inclusion of new material as with my presentation in slide nine.

### *4.2.9.7 Assessment 4: Major Project Report*

| **Coursework Example for this section.** |
|---|
| Path: \GradWith1stHons\Year 3\Major Project\Assessment4\MajorProjectReport.pdf |

This report is almost without exception, the highest weighted assessment in your degree – it is also the single biggest piece of work you will produce. My report has a total of 88 pages and is around the correct length considering it has a number of software (and VHDL source) code listings in it.

Because my report is so long (and highly technical) I am not going to provide the level of analysis given to my group project report – in fact the dissection example given in 4.2.8.3 Assessment 2: Group Project Report remains an excellent example of how a project report should be structured and is just as applicable to a Major Project report. Do of course take a good look at my Major Project report and take as much from the format as you possibly can – it is of the same standard of studentship you should be aiming for.

Because this project report is the biggest item of work you will produce and the mark weighting is so high, you should begin this report early in the third year. Officially I scheduled my report to begin in the second week of April, but in reality I was working on it as early as the beginning of March (possibly before), adding to it as the project developed. Another important point to mention is to pay careful attention to the report section of your project handbook that your project supervisor gives you. The graduation board is quite particular when it comes to your project report and as I can only advise you relative to my experience, anything that you read that conflicts with my advice is of course overruled by the handbook. So take the advice of the handbook first and my advice second.

We will now discuss a number of important items to include in the report and then finish with a number of tips that will aid you in producing your report to a high standard:

### 4.2.9.7.1 Front cover page

This page is in addition to the title page and the text is positioned so as to appear through a cut out window behind the hard binder covers of the report. The layout is as follows (font sizes 14, 18 bold and 14, Times New Roman or adjust to fit window if this is too big):

---

Derek Pell

## Low Power Consumption Digital Filters Using Primitive Operator Arithmetic

BEng Computer Systems and Electronics

---

This means your title page now falls on page 2, thus you will have no way of hiding the page number or header and footer in MS Word. The best cheat to get around this is to draw two rectangles on the page and then drag and position one rectangle over the header and the other over the footer and the page number. Now set the border and fill colour of both to white, this will hide the rectangles and more importantly, what is under them. If you are using a version of Word after 2000 you will need to select Tools/Options from the menu and turn off 'Automatically create drawing canvas when inserting AutoShapes' on the General tab.

## 4.2.9.7.2 Abstract

The abstract is a very important component of the project report and your project supervisor will stress it as such. Essentially this is a condensed introduction and conclusion in one. That is, it explains the purpose of the project and provides an outline of what was implemented in order that the project took place and finishes by summarising the outcome, and then quickly concludes. In essence, it is your project in a nutshell. Typically, the Abstract will be no more than 300 words in two paragraphs. Your project handbook will quote the number of words, so do check it first.

## 4.2.9.7.3 Notations

After your Contents, Table of Figures and Table of Tables headings and before the Introduction you must include a list of any symbols and/or abbreviations used throughout your report. This should be titled 'Notations' or less you are instructed to use another title. For example:

| Notations example | |
|---|---|
| ADC | Analogue to Digital Converter |
| BCLA | Block Carry Look Ahead |
| CLA | Carry Look Ahead |
| DSP | Digital Signal Processing etc. |

**Table 27. Example of notations for abbreviations**

Remember, it is good practice to write the full term first and then the abbreviation afterwards between brackets even though you are including a Notations list. E.g. 'my Networking assignment compares the Routing Information Protocol (RIP) and Enhanced Interior Gateway Routing Protocol (EIGRP) routing protocols performance...'

## 4.2.9.7.4 Future Work

You may wish (or be asked) to include a 'Future Work' section within your Conclusion chapter – again, see my report for an example. Typically a Future Work section is used to provide details of any future work that could be carried out to further prove your project theories or a logical progression of your project, or something along those lines.

For some projects this section may not be applicable, but if this is asked for in the handbook it is probably worth you creating something even if it is only a refinement like adding extra features. In my project this section was very applicable and the conclusion really would have been incomplete without it.

### 4.2.9.7.5   Referencing

Referencing is another important element of the project report and it's vital to realise that this is not just a method to trace where your information came from, it's insisted upon to demonstrate that you did a decent amount of research during the course of your project. In fact, I would say that if your project is largely drawn from your own ingenuity – whilst that is highly commendable – it is worth doing some extra research after the project implementation for the sake of being able to reference more in your report. However, be sure this fits in perfectly with your text. Your supervisor is likely to reinforce the fact that good referencing increases your marks.

Now the significance of referencing is understood, let's take a look at the notation format. It is actually very straightforward: when you type the information to be referenced put a set of square brackets after the text with the appropriate reference number in it. This should also be raised from the text base, so select the bracketed number and click the superscript icon (this is a tool that can be found in the Format section when customising toolbars).

The reference is then listed under the number quoted in the 'Reference' section at the end of the document. The format the reference section typically asked for is: reference number, Author's, or editors' name(s) plus initials (Capitals), Year of Publication (in brackets), Title of book (underlined), Publisher for books, and Company, title, date cited and URL for web pages. Let's look at some examples using the paragraph below:

> "In the late 1980s David R Bull and David H Horrocks began working on a digital filtering algorithm based on primitive arithmetic operations and first released a paper in July 1987 [1].
>
> During this time... These include R Thomson and T Arslan of Edinburgh University [3], A G Dempster and M D MacLeod, of Cardiff University [2], and Dr Ian Wells of Swansea Institute of Higher Education [4]. It is believed that work in this field is presently discontinued by all of the above, but Dempster is known to have pursued... etc."

| | Major Project Report referencing example |
|---|---|
| [1] | Bull, D. R. and Horrocks, D. H., 'Reduced Complexity Digital Filtering Structures Using Primitive Operations', Electronic Letters (June 1987), Vol.23, No15, pp. 769-771. |
| [2] | Electrical and Computer Engineering. Page without title found by Google search engine, (sighted May, 32006), Available from: http://www.ece.cmu.edu/~yvoronen/homepage/mcm/synth_bib.html |
| [3] | Thomson, R. and Arslan, T. An Evolutionary Algorithm for the Multiobjective Optimisation of VLSI Primitive Operator Filters, (2002), IEEE 0-7803-7282-4/02. |
| [4] | Wells, I., Digital Filter Bank Multiplier Block Implementation, Sixth European Signal Processing Conference, Brussels, Belgium, (EURASIP, August 1992), pp. 1549-1552. |
| [5] | Pell, D. J. BEng Major Project Feasibility Report and Viva Presentation Handouts, (Dec 2005), page 8. |

**Table 28. Section of a Reference page from my Major Project Report**

The exact formats for the reference page will be given with examples in your project handbook, and you may find – as I did – that you need to improvise the layout requested with some sources. There are plenty of examples in my project report so do take a look.

A nice clean method of positioning this information in the reference section is to use an invisible two column table with a narrow column on the left as demonstrated above in Table 28. To make the table invisible you need to select the table by the top left corner and select Table/Table AutoFormat... from the main menu. Once in Table AutoFormat dialog check that Table Grid is selected in the 'Table styles:' window and click on the Modify... button. Now click the grid button dropdown along the middle of the dialog. Finally, select No Border from the dropdown, and then click OK and Apply buttons to close the respective dialogs. You will still be able to see the table displayed in grey border and lines but when you print the report it will not be visible and you will be left with a clean and precise reference section.

### *4.2.9.7.6     Appendices*

In most cases you will also be required to provide an 'Appendices' and you should refer to your project handbook for instruction concerning this section as it is liable to variation. In my case the Appendices was simply a list of references to appropriate directories on a CD with all (or most) of my project source files placed inside. See my report – unfortunately I no longer have the CD, but by the time you finish your report you will have plenty of source files to arrange on a CD if that is what is required.

### 4.2.9.7.7  My tips for a good report

As stated, my report is too long for a full analysis, but here is a list of tips that my report adheres to. These tips also included references to one or two assignments to demonstrate useful techniques.

1. If you have not already done so, in MS Word, select View/Toolbars/Drawing from the main menu. Position the toolbar somewhere comfortable for you when working on documents. At the bottom above the status panel is a good choice. You are likely to need these drawing tools a lot so you may as well have them to hand.

2. Include pictorial diagrams where they are helpful in gaining understanding of material presented. Generally, include as many as needed to address all the prominent aspects of the project document and label them Figure 1, 2, etc. using the insert Caption (Insert/Reference/Caption) tool. The text that falls either before or after should of course relate to the figure concerned depending on whether it is more fitting to give a degree of explanation leading into showing the diagram, or more fitting to end one aspect and begin another with a diagram which you then explain. You should include a table of figures under the Contents index (Insert/References/Index and Table, Table of Figures tab).

3. There are a number of ways of creating pictorial diagrams, my personal favourite is Paint Shop Pro for the more complicated diagrams as it's a proper (but easy to use) graphics program that produces GIFs or JPEGs for importing into MS Word. Simple diagrams can be produced with the drawing toolbar in Word itself. It helps to make good use of the group, layering and behind/in front of text tools. Often when using the Word graphics tools you will want to turn off the Snap objects to grid option. It is suggested you customise the drawing toolbar (menu: Tools/Customize) to include the grid tool and others (you will find all drawing tools in the Command tab within the Drawing category).

4. One of the most useful methods of creating diagrams – or more accurately, computer program still shots – is the Alt + Print Screen

keys on your keyboard. If you're using a computer program like MatLab to design a computer model, you can grab the current window as a clipboard graphic using these keys at convenient stages throughout your design. You can then paste this image into your drawing software and annotate it ready for the write up in Word. This method makes really good diagrams. You may not need to annotate them, but you should use the drawing software to crop them to size. Remember a fair amount of text was spent discussing 'working smart'? Say you are modelling in MatLab prior to your project write up; using this window snapshot technique you can have all of your MatLab diagrams ready to start your write up at a later date saving valuable time. You will see how effective this technique is when looking at my work.

5. If needed you can use floating label explanations to explain aspects of your diagrams. Do this by placing text in a textbox and positioning it in white space a little away from the diagram. You need to format the textbox boarder to get rid of the line around the outside of the box (select the textbox by clicking at the edge and right click over the box and select Format Textbox, then adjust the Line Color option to None). Now you can draw an arrow from the floating label to the corresponding aspect on the diagram; the arrow can be found on the drawing toolbar. If you are annotating a GIF or JPEG (as apposed to an image drawn in Word) in this way you will need to select Tools/ Options from the menu and turn off 'Automatically create drawing canvas when inserting AutoShapes' on the General tab.

6. Also use floating textboxes with arrows pointing to text listing (the process is the same as explained in 5.) in any computer program listings that flow from page to page and anywhere else you think floating labels would help. My Digital Systems Synthesis assignment '4by4Multiplier.pdf' makes good uses of this technique, but it can prove impractical to use them if the width of the program listing is too long. Instead paragraphs in between segments of code can be used for explanation. You may even want to combine both methods in places where needed.

7. Staying on the subject of computer program listings, make sure they are well commented throughout (see my code listings for good commenting practices). When you insert listings into Word and split

them up into sections for explanation you can highlight the different components of the code and change them to the same colours they would appear in the programming editor. Again, these methods (and variations of them) are used in my C++ Object Oriented Programming assignment and group project report.

8. Try and simplify your explanations of diagrams or something technical as much as possible without leaving out information. Your explanations should be easy to follow whilst still imparting the elegance of your overall solution, design or wherever is being explained.

9. If you are taking a subject that involves a lot of maths equations use the Equation Editor in Word rather than attempt to type them on the page white space. It looks far more professional. It is suggested you select Tools/Customise from the Word menu and under Commands/Insert, drag the Equation Editor icon onto a toolbar. You can also reach it via Insert/Object on the menu.

10. Include a Bibliography section at the end of your report if it is asked for in your project hand book. The requirement for this may differ in various universities as some will not ask for it or will make it an option as a Reference section is generally required, which is a stricter version of a bibliography. You should begin with a bibliography heading when you start your report and add the source of any research you include throughout your text as you progress, otherwise you are liable to forget. Research included in your report needs to be written in your own words. See 4.2.8.3 Assessment 2: Group Project Report item 10 for deeper instructions regarding creating a bibliography.

11. Make good use of tables in your write up. Lecturers like tables that present information in an easy to understand format. Always begin your tables by making an assessment of how many columns and rows you will need and then create the table. You will probably need to improvise your tables, so select View/Toolbars/Table and Borders from the menu and doc the toolbar somewhere convenient.

12. Make good use of colours in diagrams and to highlight important computer print out text if applicable. In my group project report (see 4.2.8 Group Project for the file path) colour is use in a program listing

so that the code appears as it would in the editor allowing the variables and commands to stand out easily. With diagrams you can also use colours to create key maps making your diagrams easier to read; see pages 26 and 27 of my Major Project report for an example (see 4.2.9 Major Project for the file path). There are plenty of examples of colour in diagrams throughout my work.

13. Use the header and footer on each page and page numbers, but not on the cover or title page. The header should display the title of your project and the footer should display the course title and subject, i.e. 'Major Project'– this will ensure a professional appearance. Access the header and footer via the View menu and the page number via the Insert menu. On the Page Numbers window you need to make sure the Show numbers on first page checkbox is unchecked – this will keep both the number and the header and footer from being displayed on the cover page. Because the title page is now on page two you should use the square drawing tool and draw a rectangle over the header, footer and the page number. Again you will need to turn off the 'Automatically create drawing canvas when inserting AutoShapes'. Finally format each box so it is a solid without an outline thereby hiding the unwanted items.

14. Always present your project report with a nice clean and balanced title page. The format should be as follows: Project title (48pt or smaller if the title is longer and takes up more than two lines at 48pt, I had to use 3 lines at 36pt), your course title (20pt), the subject, i.e. 'Major Project' (20pt), the university or institute name (20pt), the date, month in words and the year in full (14pt), the word 'Author:' and your name (14pt) and the words 'Project Supervisor:' and the name of the lecturer (14pt), all centred. The two names should be near the bottom right of the page. Finally you may be asked to add the words: 'This project is submitted in partial submission for the degree concerned' (12pt centred on last line).

15. Always start your report with an Introduction and finish with a Conclusion. The introduction will introduce the project and set the document up for the explanations and descriptions to follow. The conclusion assess the techniques used to solve or construct your project and the level of success you achieved – it should also touch on

important or key elements of the project. In the conclusion you will probably also need to include a Future Work section as discussed earlier in 4.2.9.7.4 Future Work.

16. The main body chapters should be arranged in a logical order, and or less there is good reason to deviate, it is best to organise the layout as the project evolved from start to finish.

17. When using abbreviations it is good practice to write the term in full first and then put the abbreviation afterwards between brackets. E.g. Routing Information Protocol (RIP) and Enhanced Interior Gateway Routing Protocol (EIGRP). After each term has been written once in full and the abbreviation has been placed between brackets you should then just use the abbreviation from then on. You will also need to include a 'Notations' section, see 4.2.9.7.3 Notations for details.

### *4.2.9.8 Assessment 5: Exhibition*

There really isn't that much I can share with you about this one; your project supervisor will tell you what is expected. I was asked to make a poster type display of what my project was and what I accomplished etc. – if my memory serves correctly, I used twelve or so of my Final Viva presentation slides stuck to a piece of one meter square black card I was given. It really was that simple, that much I remember for sure.

# Conclusion

In this book, the mindset and strategy required to achieve a First Class degree have been discussed in detail, and examples of coursework have been provided and examined. All the knowledge and key elements are now in place and it is up to you to follow this template of success. You do not need to be a genius or possess intelligence beyond that which is of average, but you do need to have the correct attitude (mindset), be organised (strategy) and know your subject reasonably well to attain the consistent marks required to achieve a First. Always remember, many above average students, even those known to possess high IQ quotients, gain degrees of 2:1 and below every year because they were disorganised or failed to aspire towards the ranks of the First Class graduate.

Never lose sight of your goal. Know that when you are struggling with understanding or to meet deadlines, many student who achieve a First experience similar challenges, but with persistence, understanding is only ever around the corner. And it's amazing how much work you get done when you choose not to focus on the volume of your workload and just get on with it.

Achieving a First is within your reach. By purchasing this publication you have already demonstrated that you are motivated – all you have to do now is put this information into practice and be a good student. In essence being a good student is what we have been discussing throughout and that is really all there is to achieving a First. Once you know and understand what it is to be a good student and stick with that discipline there is nothing that can really stop you.

I wish you every success with your degree and in achieving First Class Honours.

# 6. Notes

Before proceeding further with this book it is very important that you read the following notes.

## Scope: which degree students will benefit from reading this?

This publication is geared towards students that study full time for three years or less (in the case of students that gain a level of exemption) to complete a Bachelor's degree. If you are studying part time or through Open University for a degree there is still a lot of relevant and valuable information in this publication that can help you achieve a First, but the information will have to be applied relative to your study situations.

## Classification – UK Bachelor's

This book is for students studying for a UK Bachelor's degree of all classifications.

## Course updates

Any updates to coursework will be uploaded directly to the coursework section of the 1stAcademy website. Notification of additions (such as additional essays), changes or news will be announced at the URL overleaf. Please check this periodically.

http://www.1stacademy.net/updates.php

Should you have any questions or feel something needs clarification, please get in touch with me via email and I will work towards any updates should it be required.

Email: derek@1stacademy.net

## Coursework example limitations

The coursework on the 1stAcademy website is included with this publication as examples of depth and quality of content you should aim towards when producing essays, assignments, project reports and presentation slides. There are also various other files like C++ program source code etc. All of this work is intended to help you with your degree, primarily as examples, but there may be aspects of this work that answers an aspect of your work. This is OK, if (say) part of a circuit design in one of the assignments can be implemented into a design of your own in order to complete your overall item. If you do use aspects of these examples do remember to reference them as instructed within this book.

What you cannot do – and I'm sure this goes without saying – is copy any item or any other author's work in its entirety. Universities frown on plagiarism and if caught students run the risk of being terminated from their course and even banned from re-entering higher education. Plagiarism includes copying information from the internet as many websites are now regarded as equivalent publication vehicles to books, papers and magazines.

In general, these examples, books and website material should be regarded as research only, whereby you take the time to understand it and are able to sculpture the material into your own words. Having done this it is vital to make the correct citations in the footnote or reference and/or bibliography sections of your coursework assessment.

# Bibliography

http://turnitin.com/static/index.html

http://www.howtogetafirst.co.uk/how-many-students-get-a-first-class-degree/

http://www.myfavoriteezines.com/articles/coaching/success-mindset-simple-how-to.html

http://www.howtogetafirst.co.uk/what-marks-are-needed-for-a-first-class-degree-or-a-21/

http://en.wikipedia.org/wiki/British_undergraduate_degree_classification

http://www.coachr.org/build_confidence_with_affirmations_and_self_talk.htm

http://en.wikipedia.org/wiki/Bachelor%27s_degree

http://en.wikipedia.org/wiki/Academic_grading_in_North_America#Grade_point_average

http://www.direct.gov.uk/en/EducationAndLearning/QualificationsExplained/DG_10039030

http://www.indicareer.com/study-abroad/educational-system-in-usa.html

http://www.stars.rdg.ac.uk/viva.html